INTERACTIVE BIBLE STUDIES

By Lyman Coleman

45 GUIDED QUESTIONNAIRES FOR GROUP BUILDING

SERENDIPITY / Box 1012 / Littleton, CO 80160 / 1-800-525-9563
www.serendipityhouse.com

97 98 99 / **CHG** / 4 3 2 1

Introduction

Welcome to Serendipity.

Serendipity happens when a few people get
together in a small group and get to know one
another, and the Holy Spirit gets
involved in the process—and something beautiful happens. It is one surprise after another. It's serendipity!

These Bible studies have been designed to let
this happen. Unlike individual Bible study,
these studies are written for small groups. The
purpose of these studies is to enable sharing in
which Scripture intersects the story in your own
life right now.

The sharing is facilitated by a questionnaire
with multiple-choice options. The questions are open-ended and there
are no right answers. In your group, you can have people with a lot of
Bible knowledge and others with no Bible knowledge.

Here's to your group. Here's to the possibility of beautiful things happening. Here's to the God of Scripture. Here's to the serendipity of the
Holy Spirit when two or three are gathered together in His name to
share life together.

Tips for Making It Happen in Your Small Group

SIZE OF GROUP. The best size of group for this kind of Bible study is four to six people. If you have more than this number, subdivide into groups of four and rearrange your chairs—close together.

TIME. These Bible studies are designed for 20 to 30 minutes. If you have less than 20 minutes, you can speed up the process by rotating around the group, letting one person answer question #1, the next person answering #2, etc.

LEADERSHIP. The questionnaire serves as the leader in the group. All you need is a convener to start the group and read the Scripture passage out loud.

SETTING. Ask the group to sit close together. The distance between their noses is the distance of the relationship. Ninety percent of communication is non-verbal. Make sure everyone can see the others.

PRAYER. The questionnaire naturally leads into sharing in prayer at the close. You can call all of the groups back together at the close for a time of prayer, or you can let each group of four conclude their own sharing with prayer. Here are three suggestions for prayer.

- Prayer Requests: Ask everyone to answer the question, "How can we help you this week in prayer?"

- Finish the Sentence: Ask everyone to finish the sentence, "God, I want to thank you for ..."

- Pray for the Person on Your Right: Go around and let everyone fill in this prayer, "Dear God, this is _____(your name), I want to thank you for _____ (person on your right) and ask you _____" (something for this person).

TABLE OF CONTENTS

Page

IDENTITY

RELATIONSHIPS

CARING

TABLE OF CONTENTS (cont.)

Page

VALUES

PRESSURES

ISSUES

TABLE OF CONTENTS (cont.)

SPIRITUAL FORMATION

BELIEFS

DISCIPLESHIP

IDENTITY

MY UNIQUENESS

Introduction

You will be looking at one of the most exciting stories in the Bible—the story of the "little guy" up a tree who Jesus picked out of the crowd because he was special and didn't know it. This man, though a Jew, was a tax collector for the ruling Romans. In those days, tax collectors were hated even more than they are today—because they were known for cheating and were considered traitors.

We recommend that you move into groups of 4 because it is easier to discuss things when you are in a smaller group—and you can finish the discussion in 30 minutes. Now, listen to the Bible story. Then, quickly move into groups of 4 and discuss the questionnaire.

ZACCHAEUS THE TAX COLLECTOR

19 *Jesus entered Jericho and was passing through. ²A man was there by the name of Zacchaeus; he was a chief tax collector and was wealthy. ³He wanted to see who Jesus was, but being a short man he could not, because of the crowd. ⁴So he ran ahead and climbed a sycamore-fig tree to see him, since Jesus was coming that way.*

⁵When Jesus reached the spot, he looked up and said to him, "Zacchaeus, come down immediately. I must stay at your house today." ⁶So he came down at once and welcomed him gladly.

⁷All the people saw this and began to mutter, "He has gone to be the guest of a 'sinner.' "

⁸But Zacchaeus stood up and said to the Lord, "Look, Lord! Here and now I give half of my possessions to the poor, and if I have cheated anybody out of anything, I will pay back four times the amount."

⁹Jesus said to him, "Today salvation has come to this house, because this man, too, is a son of Abraham. ¹⁰For the Son of Man came to seek and to save what was lost."

Luke 19:1–10

1. If you were going to make a movie about this Bible story, who would you choose to play the part of Zacchaeus—the little guy/tax collector up a tree?
   - ❏ Danny DeVito
   - ❏ Tim Allen
   - ❏ Martin Short
   - ❏ Jay Leno
   - ❏ Robin Williams
   - ❏ Jim Carey
   - ❏ Jerry Seinfeld

2. If you had been Zacchaeus when Jesus stopped under his tree and told him to "come down immediately," how would you feel?
   ❏ scared spitless
   ❏ special
   ❏ embarrassed
   ❏ suspicious
   ❏ surprised that he knew my name

3. If you had been Zacchaeus at the end of the story, how would you feel?
   ❏ clean inside
   ❏ loved
   ❏ included in God's family
   ❏ broke
   ❏ brand new

4. Jesus saw the positive qualities in Zacchaeus. Who really affirmed you when you were a kid and felt like a "little guy up a tree"?
   ❏ my mother
   ❏ my father
   ❏ my brother or sister
   ❏ another family member
   ❏ a close friend
   ❏ a teacher or coach
   ❏ a special person at church
   ❏ other: _____

5. How do the various people in your life see you now? Choose one or two of the following, and give two adjectives. For instance, "MY PARENTS see me as ... immature and rebellious."

   • MY PARENTS / SPOUSE see me as ... (two adjectives)

   • MY TEACHERS / SUPERVISORS see me as ...

   • MY CLOSE FRIENDS see me as ...

   • PEOPLE WHO DON'T KNOW ME VERY WELL see me as ...

6. In all honesty, how do you see yourself right now? Put an **"X"** on the lines below.

   I put myself down. _____I build myself up.
   (I'm no good and   (I am created in the
   never will be.)   image of God.)

   self-defeating attitude_____self-confident attitude
   (I don't want to try   (I can do everything
   because I know I'll fail.)   through Christ.)

7. Where do you put yourself "down"?
   - ☐ knowledge—"I'm not as smart as ..."
   - ☐ looks—"I'm not as good-looking as ..."
   - ☐ willpower—"I'm not as strong as ..."
   - ☐ success—"I'm not as successful as ..."
   - ☐ personality—"I'm not as well-liked as ..."
   - ☐ physical fitness—"I'm not in as good of shape as ..."
   - ☐ abilities—"I'm not as talented as ..."

8. How do you feel about sharing personal things in your life with others?
   - ☐ uncomfortable–I don't talk about these things.
   - ☐ scared–I don't know if I want to talk about these things.
   - ☐ fine–No problem, our group trusts each other.
   - ☐ thrilled–I love this stuff!
   - ☐ I'm not sure.

9. On a scale of 1 (TERRIBLE) to 10 (GREAT), how would you describe the last week? How can this group pray for you?

IDENTITY

MY PERSONALITY

Introduction

It is hard to believe that you can have two totally different personalities in the same family, but this seems to be the case in the Bible story you will be studying. The scene is the home of sisters Martha and Mary (and their brother Lazarus, whom Jesus would later raise from the dead). It seems that Jesus spent time in their home frequently.

After someone has read the Scripture passage, get into groups of 4 and discuss the questionnaire. Remember, there are no right or wrong answers—just your opinion—so you don't have to be afraid to share.

AT THE HOME OF MARTHA AND MARY

[38]As Jesus and his disciples were on their way, he came to a village where a woman named Martha opened her home to him. [39]She had a sister called Mary, who sat at the Lord's feet listening to what he said. [40]But Martha was distracted by all the preparations that had to be made. She came to him and asked, "Lord, don't you care that my sister has left me to do the work by myself? Tell her to help me!"

[41]"Martha, Martha," the Lord answered, "you are worried and upset about many things, [42]but only one thing is needed. Mary has chosen what is better, and it will not be taken away from her."

Luke 10:38–42

1. Judging by the way the two sisters acted in this story, which would you say was the older sister?
   ❏ Mary   ❏ Martha

2. If you had been Martha, how would you have responded to Jesus' remark?
   ❏ gone to my room and pouted
   ❏ thought to myself: "He doesn't have to live with my sister."
   ❏ flown off the handle
   ❏ accepted the correction, sat down with Mary, and let the supper burn

3. If you could choose one of these types of people for these situations, who would you choose? Finish the sentences by inserting either Mary ... or Martha.
   • For a close friend, I would choose ...
   • For someone to work for, I would choose ...
   • For someone to work for me, I would choose ...
   • For someone to look after my estate, I would choose ...
   • For my small group leader or youth leader, I would choose ...

4. Comparing your personality to the two people in this story, which of them are you more like?

☐ Martha—responsible and uptight

☐ Mary—carefree and laid-back

5. Who do people say you take after in your personality—your father or your mother? Which one do you think you take after?

6. Of the four classic personality types below, which type do you resemble? Read over all four types, and choose two that describe you: (a) Your dominant type, (b) Your secondary type.

Finish the sentence: *I am mostly the* _____ *type and a little bit of the* _____ *type.*

SANGUINE: People centered. Warm. Outgoing. Sociable. A good salesperson. Loves parties and shopping—just about anything that has to do with people.

CHOLERIC: Task centered. Strong-willed. Natural born leader. Loves challenges. Responsible. Good at making things happen. Likes to win. Takes chances.

MELANCHOLIC: Feelings centered. Sensitive. Introspective. Creative. Artistic. Lover of peace and quiet. Good dreamer. Writer. Expresses self in poetry.

PHLEGMATIC: Team centered. Dependable. Consistent. Organized. Good at getting things done. Methodical. Loves a neat room, a clean car, and running around with people who are the opposite.

7. If you could change something about your personality, what would it be?

8. If Jesus dropped in on you, what would he point out that distracts *you* from the most important things in life?

9. How could others in your group or church help you in this?
   - ☐ by helping me understand what is going on inside of me
   - ☐ by leaving me alone
   - ☐ by telling me it's okay to be me
   - ☐ by sharing some of their own struggles
   - ☐ by challenging me to be all that I can be
   - ☐ other:_____

10. Jesus said Martha was "worried and upset about many things." What are you worried or upset about right now?

11. How can this group remember you in prayer this week?

IDENTITY

MY VALUES

Introduction
This is the story of a young ruler who came to Jesus to ask what he could do to receive eternal life. He must have come from a rich family because he had "great wealth" at an early age. Jesus "threw him a curve" and asked him to sell everything and give the money to the poor.

The questionnaire below is going to ask you some hard questions. Get into groups of 4 and have someone read the Scripture out loud.

THE RICH RULER
[18]A certain ruler asked him, "Good teacher, what must I do to inherit eternal life?"

[19]"Why do you call me good?" Jesus answered. "No one is good—except God alone. [20]You know the commandments: 'Do not commit adultery, do not murder, do not steal, do not give false testimony, honor your father and mother.' "

[21]"All these I have kept since I was a boy," he said.

[22]When Jesus heard this, he said to him, "You still lack one thing. Sell everything you have and give to the poor, and you will have treasure in heaven. Then come, follow me."

[23]When he heard this, he became very sad, because he was a man of great wealth. [24]Jesus looked at him and said, "How hard it is for the rich to enter the kingdom of God! [25]Indeed, it is easier for a camel to go through the eye of a needle than for a rich man to enter the kingdom of God."

[26]Those who heard this asked, "Who then can be saved?"

[27]Jesus replied, "What is impossible with men is possible with God."

Luke 18:18–27

1. If the rich young man in this Bible story lived today, how would he dress?
   ❐ sharp and conservative
   ❐ in the latest far-out fashions
   ❐ in jeans and a T-shirt

2. If this person came to your church, how would he be treated?
   ❐ We would probably be impressed.
   ❐ Our treasurer would be thrilled.
   ❐ We would accept him as a person and not care at all about his money.
   ❐ We would expect more out of him because of his money.

3. How do you feel about the rich young ruler?
   - ❐ sorry for him—He couldn't help it that he was rich.
   - ❐ disappointed in him—He walked away from God.
   - ❐ upset—Jesus should not have been so hard on him.
   - ❐ frustrated—Does this mean I have to give up everything I have, too?

4. What would you do if Jesus asked you to sell everything you had and give the proceeds to the poor?
   - ❐ have my hearing checked
   - ❐ compute my net worth and think about it
   - ❐ hold a garage sale this Saturday
   - ❐ increase my giving to the church
   - ❐ sadly walk away

5. Being totally honest, what are your top three priorities in life now?
   - ❐ a good time
   - ❐ good friendships
   - ❐ a good marriage / family
   - ❐ making lots of money
   - ❐ greater intimacy with God
   - ❐ having nice things
   - ❐ financial independence / security
   - ❐ being true to myself
   - ❐ developing my spiritual gifts
   - ❐ making a contribution to the world
   - ❐ other:_____

6. Right now, who influences you most on your values?
   - ❐ my peers
   - ❐ my pastor / church
   - ❐ my parents / grandparents
   - ❐ my spouse / boyfriend / girlfriend
   - ❐ the media / TV

7. How much has your commitment to Jesus Christ and his way of life influenced your values?
   - ❐ a lot
   - ❐ a little
   - ❐ not as much as I would like
   - ❐ not at all

8. Jesus knew that the young ruler's riches were a barrier between him and God. If Jesus were to evaluate your life, what would he say holds you back from being totally committed to God?
   - ❏ wealth
   - ❏ apathy
   - ❏ habit or temptations
   - ❏ doubts about issues of faith
   - ❏ fear of being labeled a fanatic
   - ❏ other:_____

9. What do you need to do to store up "treasure in heaven"?
   - ❏ Cut back on my lifestyle.
   - ❏ Invest more time in loving people and less in loving things.
   - ❏ Overhaul my priorities.
   - ❏ Talk to more people about Christ.
   - ❏ Spend more time at church.
   - ❏ Keep doing what I'm already doing.
   - ❏ other:_____

10. How would you like the group to pray for you?

MY ABILITIES

Introduction

Can one person make a difference in this world? A lot of us would say "no." In this Bible study, you will have a chance to see what Jesus did with a little ... from a few people ... to make a difference. And you will have a chance to discuss where your own gifts and abilities could make a difference.

Keep in mind that this story occurred when the disciples were on a vacation with Jesus. They had just returned from an exhausting job and Jesus invited them to take a break. As you listen to the story, try to put yourself in their situation. Then, move into groups of 4 and discuss the questionnaire.

JESUS FEEDS THE FIVE THOUSAND

30The apostles gathered around Jesus and reported to him all they had done and taught. 31Then, because so many people were coming and going that they did not even have a chance to eat, he said to them, "Come with me by yourselves to a quiet place and get some rest."

32So they went away by themselves in a boat to a solitary place. 33But many who saw them leaving recognized them and ran on foot from all the towns and got there ahead of them. 34When Jesus landed and saw a large crowd, he had compassion on them, because they were like sheep without a shepherd. So he began teaching them many things.

35By this time it was late in the day, so his disciples came to him. "This is a remote place," they said, "and it's already very late. 36Send the people away so they can go to the surrounding countryside and villages and buy themselves something to eat."

37But he answered, "You give them something to eat."

They said to him, "That would take eight months of a man's wages! Are we to go and spend that much on bread and give it to them to eat?"

38"How many loaves do you have?" he asked. "Go and see."
When they found out, they said, "Five—and two fish."

39Then Jesus directed them to have all the people sit down in groups on the green grass. 40So they sat down in groups of hundreds and fifties. 41Taking the five loaves and the two fish and looking up to heaven, he gave thanks and broke the loaves. Then he gave them to his disciples to set before the people. He also divided the two fish among them all. 42They all ate and were satisfied, 43and the disciples picked up twelve basketfuls of broken pieces of bread and fish. 44The number of the men who had eaten was five thousand.

Mark 6:30–44

1. "Come with me by yourselves to a quiet place and get some rest." If you were one of the disciples, what would you expect?
   - ❑ a quiet little vacation
   - ❑ time to be with Jesus
   - ❑ fun and recreation
   - ❑ anything but people

2. Surprise! There are 5,000 men, plus women and children, waiting on the shore. Now how do you feel?
   - ❑ delighted
   - ❑ angry
   - ❑ overwhelmed
   - ❑ whipped
   - ❑ compassionate
   - ❑ frustrated

3. What is guaranteed to ruin a vacation for you?
   - ❑ standing in long lines
   - ❑ car trouble
   - ❑ losing my suitcase
   - ❑ mosquitoes / jellyfish / ants
   - ❑ seven straight days of rain
   - ❑ other:_____

4. "You give them something to eat." Had you been with Jesus during this story, and he asked you to do work after he promised you rest, what would have been your reaction?
   - ❑ "Okay, but you owe me one!"
   - ❑ "Hey, I'm outta here!"
   - ❑ "Whatever you say, Lord!"
   - ❑ "But you PROMISED!"

5. How much of your potential are you giving to God right now?
   - ❑ sorry you asked
   - ❑ I would say 50%.
   - ❑ maybe 5%
   - ❑ I'm giving it all I've got.

6. If you could put your gifts to work in something that you are good at, what would you like to do? (Choose two or three from the list below.)

- ❏ working with children
- ❏ listening / caring
- ❏ helping behind the scenes
- ❏ playing an instrument
- ❏ working with older people
- ❏ peacemaking / reconciling
- ❏ organizing / administering
- ❏ being sensitive to others
- ❏ sharing my faith
- ❏ motivating / leading
- ❏ crusading for a cause
- ❏ cooking / homemaking
- ❏ teaching the Bible
- ❏ writing
- ❏ getting others involved
- ❏ coaching / teaching
- ❏ raising money
- ❏ making people laugh
- ❏ acting / singing
- ❏ cheering others on
- ❏ problem solving
- ❏ other:_____

7. If you knew you could not fail, what would be one thing you would like to do with your life in the near future?

- ❏ go on a service or mission trip
- ❏ do something for the homeless
- ❏ reach out to some "problem" kids in my school or community
- ❏ get involved in an inner-city church or ministry
- ❏ lead a support or recovery group
- ❏ tutor disadvantaged kids
- ❏ help out at a hospital or nursing home
- ❏ other:_____

8. What is keeping you from doing this?

- ❏ money
- ❏ feeling inadequate
- ❏ time
- ❏ I don't know enough.
- ❏ I'm really not that committed.

9. How could this group help you get started?

- ❏ Don't push me—I was only dreaming!
- ❏ Help me think it through.
- ❏ Join me.
- ❏ Encourage me.
- ❏ Pray for me.

10. If Jesus had you sit down right where you are while he miraculously met your most immediate need, what would he do for you?

IDENTITY

MY FUTURE

Introduction

Everybody identifies with Peter. He was always outspoken and doing things that he shouldn't. But he also was someone who was willing to take risks—sometimes crazy risks. This Bible story is one of those times.

Now, move into groups of 4 and have someone read the Scripture passage out loud. Then, discuss the questionnaire.

JESUS WALKS ON THE WATER

[22]*Immediately Jesus made the disciples get into the boat and go on ahead of him to the other side, while he dismissed the crowd.* [23]*After he had dismissed them, he went up on a mountainside by himself to pray. When evening came, he was there alone,* [24]*but the boat was already a considerable distance from land, buffeted by the waves because the wind was against it.*

[25]*During the fourth watch of the night Jesus went out to them, walking on the lake.* [26]*When the disciples saw him walking on the lake, they were terrified. "It's a ghost," they said, and cried out in fear.*

[27]*But Jesus immediately said to them: "Take courage! It is I. Don't be afraid."*

[28]*"Lord, if it's you," Peter replied, "tell me to come to you on the water."*

[29]*"Come," he said.*

Then Peter got down out of the boat, walked on the water and came toward Jesus. [30]*But when he saw the wind, he was afraid and, beginning to sink, cried out, "Lord, save me!"*

[31]*Immediately Jesus reached out his hand and caught him. "You of little faith,"* *he said, "Why did you doubt?"*

[32]*And when they climbed into the boat, the wind died down.* [33]*Then those who were in the boat worshiped him, saying, "Truly you are the Son of God."*

Matthew 14:22–33

1. Imagine you were a journalist and met the disciples on the other side of the lake after this incident. What would you do next?
   - ❐ sell the story to *The National Enquirer*
   - ❐ develop a segment for *Unsolved Mysteries* on television
   - ❐ ignore it so that nobody would think I was crazy
   - ❐ gather testimony and write about it for a network news show

2. If you had been in the boat when the disciples saw someone walking on the water, what would you have said?
   - ☐ "I'm seeing things!"
   - ☐ "Where's Jesus?!"
   - ☐ "Let me out of here!"
   - ☐ "Do you see what I see?"
   - ☐ "I think I ate too many anchovies!"
   - ☐ I would have been speechless.

3. If you could put in a good word for Peter here in this story, what would you say?
   - ☐ He meant well.
   - ☐ He learned a lot from this experience.
   - ☐ He at least was willing to ask.

4. How are you at "stepping out of the boat" and taking risks?
   - ☐ just plain scared
   - ☐ I'll try anything once.
   - ☐ daring
   - ☐ I'm good at going second.
   - ☐ cautious—I put my big toe in first.

5. Where do you feel God is inviting you to get out of the boat now?
   - ☐ in my relationships—dealing with a problem
   - ☐ in my future planning—doing something I've been afraid to try
   - ☐ in my inner life—facing a hang-up
   - ☐ in my spiritual walk—putting God first

6. Before you can do this, what is standing in the way?
   - ☐ fear of failure
   - ☐ my negative thoughts
   - ☐ inconsistency
   - ☐ intellectual doubts
   - ☐ fear of standing alone
   - ☐ unhealthy relationships
   - ☐ sense of inadequacy
   - ☐ impulse to rush into things before counting the cost
   - ☐ other:_____

7. What would be the best way for God to help in the situation?
   - ❐ be very gentle with me
   - ❐ give me a good kick in the pants
   - ❐ assure me it's okay to fail
   - ❐ surround me with supportive people
   - ❐ get out of the boat with me

8. What dreams do you have for the future? What risks are involved?

9. What are you facing in your life right now that you need to hear Jesus say, "Don't be afraid"?

10. How can this group help you in prayer this week?

RELATIONSHIPS

FRIENDSHIPS

Introduction

You will be looking at the story of David and Jonathan, one of the best stories in the Bible on friendships. Jonathan was the son of King Saul. King Saul became jealous of David after David killed Goliath, and plotted to kill David. Jonathan found out about it and his friendship with David was put to the test.

Now, listen to the Bible story. Then, quickly move into groups of 4 and discuss the questionnaire.

³And Jonathan made a covenant with David because he loved him as himself. ⁴Jonathan took off the robe he was wearing and gave it to David, along with his tunic, and even his sword, his bow and his belt.

1 Samuel 18:3–4

19 *Saul told his son Jonathan and all the attendants to kill David. But Jonathan was very fond of David ²and warned him, "My father Saul is looking for a chance to kill you. Be on your guard tomorrow morning; go into hiding and stay there. ³I will go out and stand with my father in the field where you are. I'll speak to him about you and will tell you what I find out."*

⁴Jonathan spoke well of David to Saul his father and said to him, "Let not the king do wrong to his servant David; he has not wronged you, and what he has done has benefited you greatly. ⁵He took his life in his hands when he killed the Philistine. The Lord won a great victory for all Israel, and you saw it and were glad. Why then would you do wrong to an innocent man like David by killing him for no reason?"

1 Samuel 19:1–5

⁴¹After the boy had gone, David got up from the south side of the stone and bowed down before Jonathan three times, with his face to the ground. Then they kissed each other and wept together—but David wept the most.

⁴²Jonathan said to David, "Go in peace, for we have sworn friendship with each other in the name of the Lord, saying, 'The Lord is witness between you and me, and between your descendants and my descendants forever.' " Then David left, and Jonathan went back to the town.

1 Samuel 20:41–42

1. As you think about the story of David and Jonathan, what immediately comes to mind?

❏ This is beautiful.

❏ This is corny.

❏ This sounds like a Hollywood plot.

❏ I wish I had a friend like that.

2. If you had been Jonathan, and knew your father was threatening to kill your best friend, what would you have thought?

☐ There must be something wrong with my dad.
☐ There must be something wrong with my friend.
☐ There must be something wrong with me.
☐ I would feel terribly torn.

3. If you realized that your father was doing this to save the throne for you, how would you have felt?

☐ unworthy
☐ disgusted
☐ torn
☐ appreciative
☐ I would stay out of it.

4. Who was your best friend when you were a kid? What one experience did you have together that you especially remember?

5. As you think back, what was it about this person that brought the two of you together?

☐ doing fun things together
☐ liking the same things
☐ sharing personal things
☐ getting in trouble together
☐ keeping each other's confidence
☐ letting each other have space
☐ being there for each other when one of us was hurting
☐ going to church together / praying together

6. When it comes to making friends, what do you do? Finish the sentence by picking ONE in each category: "I usually ..."

make friends quickly_____slowly

change friends constantly _____never

break off friendships easily _____painfully

choose friends wisely _____unwisely

7. What qualities do you look for when you choose a friend? (Choose the top three.)
    - ❏ similar lifestyle
    - ❏ honesty
    - ❏ generosity
    - ❏ spiritual depth
    - ❏ easy to talk to
    - ❏ common interests
    - ❏ loyalty
    - ❏ good sense of humor
    - ❏ ethnic background
    - ❏ speaks his or her mind
    - ❏ other:_____

8. What is your biggest barrier to having closer friendships?
    - ❏ acting like I don't need them
    - ❏ being jealous
    - ❏ hiding my feelings
    - ❏ having been hurt in the past
    - ❏ focusing on things rather than people
    - ❏ other:_____

9. How hard is it for you to trust this group with the heavy stuff in your life? What could help?

10. How can your friends in this group pray for you right now?

RELATIONSHIPS

BEING REAL

Introduction

It's hard to love someone you do not know. And it is hard to get to know someone who wears a mask. In this Bible passage, you will meet two people who pray in different ways. As you read, remember that the Pharisee was a very religious person and the tax collector was probably the most hated person in the community.

Move into groups of 4. Then, have someone read the parable aloud and start on the questionnaire.

THE PARABLE OF THE PHARISEE AND THE TAX COLLECTOR

⁹To some who were confident of their own righteousness and looked down on everybody else, Jesus told this parable: ¹⁰"Two men went up to the temple to pray, one a Pharisee and the other a tax collector. ¹¹The Pharisee stood up and prayed about himself: 'God, I thank you that I am not like other men—robbers, evildoers, adulterers—or even like this tax collector. ¹²I fast twice a week and give a tenth of all I get.'

¹³"But the tax collector stood at a distance. He would not even look up to heaven, but beat his breast and said, 'God, have mercy on me, a sinner.'

¹⁴"I tell you that this man, rather than the other, went home justified before God. For everyone who exalts himself will be humbled, and he who humbles himself will be exalted."

Luke 18:9–14

1. How do you feel about the Pharisee in this story?
   - ❒ I feel sorry for him.
   - ❒ I feel a little angry.
   - ❒ I feel like punching him in the nose.
   - ❒ I have the same attitude that he does.

2. How do you feel about the tax collector?
   - ❒ At least he's honest.
   - ❒ I can relate to this guy.
   - ❒ After cheating people, he has some nerve!
   - ❒ I think he was being just as much of a phony as the Pharisee.

3. How much of your own problems could you share with each of these people? Put an *"X"* on the line to indicate your response—somewhere in between the two extremes.

WITH THE PHARISEE, I COULD SHARE:
Everything _____Nothing

WITH THE TAX COLLECTOR, I COULD SHARE:
Everything _____Nothing

4. For the person with whom you could share the most, why do you feel this way?
   ❑ He is more spiritual.
   ❑ He is more honest.
   ❑ He is more like me.
   ❑ He is more like the person I want to be.
   ❑ He is more likely to understand me.

5. If the tax collector in the parable came to your group or church, how would he be received?
   ❑ with open arms
   ❑ with suspicion
   ❑ with disgust
   ❑ like one of us

6. If the Pharisee in the parable showed up at your group or church, how would he be received?
   ❑ with open arms
   ❑ with raised eyebrows
   ❑ with a few snickers
   ❑ with cold stares
   ❑ with sympathy

7. How much of the Pharisee and the tax collector do you see in yourself? Put a percentage for each—and the two must add up to 100%.

   I see myself as _____% Pharisee
   and _____% tax collector.

8. Why do you think so many people confess their sins in bars rather than in churches?

9. With whom do you "get real" and share your problems?
- ❏ my spouse
- ❏ my parent(s)
- ❏ my boyfriend or girlfriend
- ❏ this group
- ❏ another family member
- ❏ a close friend
- ❏ my pastor or small group leader
- ❏ no one
- ❏ other:_____

10. How do you feel about sharing personal matters in your life with this group?
- ❏ uncomfortable—I don't talk about these things.
- ❏ scared—I don't know if I want to talk about these things.
- ❏ okay—I can handle it.
- ❏ thrilled—I love this stuff!
- ❏ I'm not sure.

11. How would you like this group to remember you in prayer this week?

RELATIONSHIPS

TRUE FRIENDS

Introduction

In this Bible study, you will meet four friends who were so concerned about the well-being of their friend that they literally "tore up the roof" for this person. After hearing the Bible story, you will have a chance to share your own feelings about "going the distance" for friends.

Now, move into groups of 4 and listen to the story. Then, discuss the following questionnaire.

JESUS HEALS A PARALYTIC

2 *A few days later, when Jesus again entered Capernaum, the people heard that he had come home. ²So many gathered that there was no room left, not even outside the door, and he preached the word to them. ³Some men came, bringing to him a paralytic, carried by four of them. ⁴Since they could not get him to Jesus because of the crowd, they made an opening in the roof above Jesus and, after digging through it, lowered the mat the paralyzed man was lying on. ⁵When Jesus saw their faith, he said to the paralytic, "Son, your sins are forgiven."*

⁶Now some teachers of the law were sitting there, thinking to themselves, ⁷"Why does this fellow talk like that? He's blaspheming! Who can forgive sins but God alone?"

⁸Immediately Jesus knew in his spirit that this was what they were thinking in their hearts, and he said to them, "Why are you thinking these things? ⁹Which is easier: to say to the paralytic, 'Your sins are forgiven,' or to say, 'Get up, take your mat and walk'? ¹⁰But that you may know that the Son of Man has authority on earth to forgive sins . . . ." He said to the paralytic, ¹¹"I tell you, get up, take your mat and go home." ¹²He got up, took his mat and walked out in full view of them all. This amazed everyone and they praised God, saying, "We have never seen anything like this!"

Mark 2:1–12

1. If CNN reported on this incident, what would be their lead line?
   - ❏ A faith healer makes a paralytic walk.
   - ❏ Four friends raise the roof to help a friend.
   - ❏ A preacher upsets religious leaders.
   - ❏ Police are looking for vandals in a house break-in.

2. If you were one of the paralytic's four friends and saw the crowd where Jesus was, what would you do?

❏ suggest we come back later

❏ politely wait in line

❏ make a hole in the roof

❏ go along with the hole in the roof, but make it clear it wasn't my idea

3. How would you feel if you were the paralytic when your friends decided to help you "drop in on Jesus"?

❏ reluctant—"You will embarrass me."

❏ scared—"You're going to drop me!"

❏ grateful—"Thanks for your concern."

❏ apprehensive—"They are going to throw us out!"

❏ mixed feelings—"I don't think this is going to work, but I will trust you guys."

4. What impresses you most about the four friends?

❏ their faith

❏ their boldness

❏ their ingenuity and creativity

❏ their determination

❏ their concern for their friend

5. What is the closest you have come to having a supportive community who cared for you when you were hurting?

6. It is 12 o'clock at night. You are in trouble. You need some friends to come over and be with you. Four friends that would:

• listen as you talk about the crisis you are going through ...

• be with you as late as necessary ...

• keep your problem confidential ...

• pray for you ...

• and support you through this crisis.

WHAT FRIENDS WOULD YOU CALL? Give four first names.

7. What event in your life brought you closest to God?
   - ❐ when some friends really supported me
   - ❐ when Jesus healed me when I was hurting
   - ❐ when someone I was close to got really sick or died
   - ❐ when I attended a camp or special worship experience
   - ❐ when I committed my life to Christ
   - ❐ when I felt God's forgiveness
   - ❐ No event has brought me that feeling.
   - ❐ other:_____

8. How do you need to change to receive more support from friends?
   - ❐ be more open
   - ❐ be a better listener
   - ❐ stop trying to be so self-sufficient
   - ❐ be more supportive myself
   - ❐ find some new or different friends
   - ❐ be more patient
   - ❐ other:_____

9. Who were the friends in your life who cared enough to bring you to Jesus?

10. If you had friends who would take you to Jesus for healing today, what kind of healing would you ask for?
   - ❐ physical
   - ❐ spiritual
   - ❐ emotional
   - ❐ relational

11. Pray about what was just shared. Then close your meeting by affirming one another. Have each person listen silently while others share what qualities that person has that make him or her a good friend.

PEER PRESSURE

Introduction

The story of the woman caught in the act of adultery is a good example of peer pressure. The Pharisees put a lot of pressure on Jesus to go along with the crowd and condemn this woman.

Listen to the story carefully. Try to put yourself in the shoes of Jesus. See how he dealt with the dilemma that he faced. Then, get together in groups of 4 and discuss the questionnaire.

THE WOMAN CAUGHT IN ADULTERY

8 *But Jesus went to the Mount of Olives. ²At dawn he appeared again in the temple courts, where all the people gathered around him, and he sat down to teach them. ³The teachers of the law and the Pharisees brought in a woman caught in adultery. They made her stand before the group ⁴and said to Jesus, "Teacher, this woman was caught in the act of adultery. ⁵In the Law Moses commanded us to stone such women. Now what do you say?" ⁶They were using this question as a trap, in order to have a basis for accusing him.*

But Jesus bent down and started to write on the ground with his finger. ⁷When they kept on questioning him, he straightened up and said to them, "If any one of you is without sin, let him be the first to throw a stone at her." ⁸Again he stooped down and wrote on the ground.

⁹At this, those who heard began to go away one at a time, the older ones first, until only Jesus was left, with the woman still standing there. ¹⁰Jesus straightened up and asked her, "Woman, where are they? Has no one condemned you?"

¹¹"No one, sir," she said.

"Then neither do I condemn you," Jesus declared, "Go now and leave your life of sin."

John 8:1–11

1. Who do you feel most sorry for in this story?
   ❑ the woman—for being publicly humiliated
   ❑ Jesus—for being pressured by the crowd
   ❑ the religious leaders—for stooping this low

2. If you had been Jesus when the woman caught in the act of adultery was brought before him, how would you have felt?
   - ❏ embarrassed
   - ❏ angry at the Pharisees
   - ❏ ashamed of the woman
   - ❏ torn between mixed feelings
   - ❏ intimidated by the Pharisees
   - ❏ mad for being put on the spot
   - ❏ sorry for the woman

3. Who do you admire for the way they don't cave in to the pressure of the crowd?

4. When it comes to going against the crowd, who are the hardest people for you to stand up against?
   - ❏ supervisors / authority figures
   - ❏ friends at school or work
   - ❏ friends at church
   - ❏ spouse / boyfriend / girlfriend
   - ❏ parents / family members
   - ❏ other:_____

5. How tough is it to face the following pressures from the crowd? Rate yourself from 1 to 10 in each category. Then, share with the group your easiest and your hardest.

ABUSING DRUGS OR ALCOHOL

| Easy | 1 | 2 | 3 | 4 | 5 | 6 | 7 | 8 | 9 | 10 | Hard |

CHEATING ON TESTS OR TAXES

| Easy | 1 | 2 | 3 | 4 | 5 | 6 | 7 | 8 | 9 | 10 | Hard |

LYING TO COVER UP WRONGDOING

| Easy | 1 | 2 | 3 | 4 | 5 | 6 | 7 | 8 | 9 | 10 | Hard |

KEEPING UP WITH FRIENDS IN MATERIAL THINGS

| Easy | 1 | 2 | 3 | 4 | 5 | 6 | 7 | 8 | 9 | 10 | Hard |

CURSING / PROFANITY / DIRTY JOKES

| Easy | 1 | 2 | 3 | 4 | 5 | 6 | 7 | 8 | 9 | 10 | Hard |

RAUNCHY MOVIES, MAGAZINES, ETC.

Easy   1   2   3   4   5   6   7   8   9   10   Hard

NOT STANDING UP FOR YOUR FAITH

Easy   1   2   3   4   5   6   7   8   9   10   Hard

6. What have you found helpful in dealing with peer pressure?
   - ❐ attend church regularly
   - ❐ study the Bible and pray
   - ❐ stay away from the wrong crowd
   - ❐ just say no
   - ❐ let others know where I stand on issues and why

7. What grade would you give your group or church on how well you support each other and stand together against peer pressure?
   - ❐ I would give us an A+.
   - ❐ Well, I'd give us a C-.
   - ❐ I'd give us a B+ for effort.
   - ❐ I'm sorry you asked.

8. If the woman who was caught in adultery came to your group or church, how would she feel?
   - ❐ weird
   - ❐ tried and convicted
   - ❐ uncomfortable at first
   - ❐ right at home

9. What do you do when you blow it?
   - ❐ crawl into a hole
   - ❐ try to be extra good
   - ❐ confess it to God and move on
   - ❐ shrug it off
   - ❐ confess it to another person

10. How does the way Jesus treated this woman help you face your sins?

11. How can the group pray for you?

RELATIONSHIPS

FAMILY EXPECTATIONS

Introduction
Your family probably has certain expectations of you. But what if they went to Jesus and asked him to make you his prime minister? In the Bible story, you will have a chance to see what happened in a situation like this and to talk about some of your own "stories."

Now, listen to the Bible story. Then, move into groups of 4 to share your responses.

A MOTHER'S REQUEST
²⁰Then the mother of Zebedee's sons came to Jesus with her sons and, kneeling down, asked a favor of him.

²¹"What is it you want?" he asked.

She said, "Grant that one of these two sons of mine may sit at your right and the other at your left in your kingdom."

²²"You don't know what you are asking," Jesus said to them. "Can you drink the cup I am going to drink?"

"We can," they answered.

²³Jesus said to them, "You will indeed drink from my cup, but to sit at my right or left is not for me to grant. These places belong to those for whom they have been prepared by my Father."

²⁴When the ten heard about this, they were indignant with the two brothers. ²⁵Jesus called them together and said, "You know that the rulers of the Gentiles lord it over them, and their high officials exercise authority over them. ²⁶Not so with you. Instead, whoever wants to become great among you must be your servant, ²⁷and whoever wants to be first must be your slave—²⁸just as the Son of Man did not come to be served, but to serve, and to give his life as a ransom for many."

Matthew 20:20–28

1. If you were one of these two brothers, how would you have felt about your mother's request at the beginning of this story?
   ❐ embarrassed
   ❐ honored
   ❐ angry

2. How would you have felt at the end of the story?
   - ❑ humiliated
   - ❑ mad at my mother
   - ❑ grateful for the lesson I learned
   - ❑ disappointed in Jesus
   - ❑ afraid the other disciples would hold a grudge against me

3. These brothers turned out to be significant leaders in the church. How much credit do you give their mother for this?
   - ❑ a whole lot
   - ❑ a little
   - ❑ none

4. What did your parents expect you to do when you were young?
   - ❑ play a musical instrument
   - ❑ compete in sports
   - ❑ make good grades
   - ❑ "be seen and not heard"
   - ❑ do lots of chores
   - ❑ other:_____

5. Which of the following comes closest to the truth concerning your family's expectations for you?
   - ❑ My family expects very little—I wonder if they even care.
   - ❑ My family expects too much—I can never live up to their expectations.
   - ❑ My family's expectations are high enough to challenge me, but not too high to discourage me.
   - ❑ My family has helped me to set my own expectations.

6. Are you living up to your family's expectations?
   - ❑ Are you kidding?!
   - ❑ I'm trying.
   - ❑ I quit trying.
   - ❑ Yes.
   - ❑ I think I am exceeding their expectations for me.

7. How do (or will) you let your children know your expectations for them?
   - ❑ I (will) let my kids set their own rules.
   - ❑ I (will) sit down with my kids and explain things.
   - ❑ I (will) spend extra time with my kids.
   - ❑ I (will) teach my kids by example.
   - ❑ other:_____

8. When you have a difference with a family member over expectations, what have you found helpful?
   - ❒ I take the opportunity to sit down and talk.
   - ❒ I tell them what they want to hear and forget it.
   - ❒ I try to see where they are coming from.
   - ❒ I try to help us come up with a compromise together.
   - ❒ I put expectations in writing to prevent such problems.
   - ❒ other:_____

9. What issues cause the greatest conflict between you and other family members? (Choose the top three.)

   ___ household duties   ___ discipline

   ___ work schedules   ___ drugs / alcohol

   ___ leisure time / activities   ___ manners

   ___ going to church   ___ language

   ___ clothes / hairstyle   ___ respect

   ___ other relatives / in-laws   ___ money

   ___ future plans   ___ music preferences

   ___ friends   ___ favoritism

   ___ school / grades   ___ curfew

10. For the three issues you just identified, who do you think causes the problem? For each issue, put one of these symbols:

    M = Me (It's my problem or I cause it.)

    F = Family Member (It's their problem or they cause it.)

    O = Other (Someone or something else causes the problem.)

11. How can this group help you in prayer this week?

CARING

TOUGH LOVE

Introduction
This Bible story is about a disabled person who waited hopefully at a pool that had a reputation of healing the first person who got in when the water was stirred. Jesus stopped to talk to this man and asked him a very interesting question: "Do you want to get well?"

Listen to this story as it is read. Then, move into groups of 4 and discuss the questionnaire.

THE HEALING AT THE POOL
5 *Some time later, Jesus went up to Jerusalem for a feast of the Jews. ²Now there is in Jerusalem near the Sheep Gate a pool, which in Aramaic is called Bethesda and which is surrounded by five covered colonnades. ³Here a great number of disabled people used to lie—the blind, the lame, the paralyzed. ⁵One who was there had been an invalid for thirty-eight years. ⁶When Jesus saw him lying there and learned that he had been in this condition for a long time, he asked him, "Do you want to get well?"*

⁷"Sir," the invalid replied, "I have no one to help me into the pool when the water is stirred. While I am trying to get in, someone else goes down ahead of me."

⁸Then Jesus said to him, "Get up! Pick up your mat and walk." ⁹At once the man was cured; he picked up his mat and walked.

The day on which this took place was a Sabbath, ¹⁰and so the Jews said to the man who had been healed, "It is the Sabbath; the law forbids you to carry your mat."

¹¹But he replied, "The man who made me well said to me, 'Pick up your mat and walk.' "

¹²So they asked him, "Who is this fellow who told you to pick it up and walk?"

¹³The man who was healed had no idea who it was, for Jesus had slipped away into the crowd that was there.

¹⁴Later Jesus found him at the temple and said to him, "See, you are well again. Stop sinning or something worse may happen to you." ¹⁵The man went away and told the Jews that it was Jesus who had made him well.

John 5:1–15

1. How would you feel if you had been disabled for 38 years like the man in this story?
   ❑ helpless and dependent
   ❑ bitter and angry
   ❑ discouraged and depressed
   ❑ accepting of my condition

2. How would you have felt when Jesus asked you, "Do you want to get well?"
   - ❏ insulted
   - ❏ challenged
   - ❏ hopeful
   - ❏ cared for
   - ❏ mocked
   - ❏ cynical

3. Where is the "watering hole" for the dropouts in your school or community?

4. If Jesus asked these people, "Do you want to get well?" what would they say?
   - ❏ "I want to get well, but my friends won't help me."
   - ❏ "My parents have ruined my life."
   - ❏ "I have a learning disability."
   - ❏ "I was abused as a child."
   - ❏ "I can't break my addiction."
   - ❏ "My gang would kill me if I left."
   - ❏ "I'm not sick!"

5. Who has shown you "tough love"?
   - ❏ my father
   - ❏ my mother
   - ❏ a teacher
   - ❏ a coach
   - ❏ my brother / sister
   - ❏ a friend
   - ❏ another family member
   - ❏ a counselor
   - ❏ a pastor / group leader
   - ❏ a group like this

6. How well do you accept tough love? How well do you show tough love to others?

7. What is the closest Jesus has come to saying to you, "Get up! Pick up your mat and walk"?
   - ❏ when I turned my life over to him
   - ❏ when I experienced his healing
   - ❏ when I had a self-pity problem
   - ❏ when I was overly dependent on others
   - ❏ when I lost my will to get better
   - ❏ other:_____

8. If Jesus were to stop by the "watering hole" where you hang out, what would he probably ask you?

☐ "Do you want to get well?"

☐ "What are you doing with your life?"

☐ "Are you satisfied with what you are doing?"

☐ "Are you looking for the real thing?"

☐ "When will you quit complaining and be content?"

9. When you go through something that leaves you feeling like a cripple, what have you found helpful?

☐ time alone with God

☐ talking things over with a friend

☐ getting back into a spiritual discipline

☐ being in a group or church like this

☐ listening to music

☐ getting a good night's sleep

☐ admitting I have blown it and getting on with life

10. What connection between your physical and spiritual health have you noticed? When do you find yourself getting physically sick over problems in other areas of your life?

11. What ailments—physical, spiritual or otherwise—does Jesus need to treat in your life?

CARING

DOWN AND DIRTY

Introduction

Where would you look in the Bible for a model of true caring? This story occurs during a special meal Jesus ate with his disciples on the night before his death. It was customary for people's dusty, sandaled feet to be washed, usually by the lowest ranking servant, before a meal was served.

Listen to the story. Imagine yourself sitting there as the tension mounts. Watch Jesus as he gets up ... takes off his garment ... wraps a towel around his waist ... and begins to wash ... your feet. Then, move into groups of 4 and discuss the questionnaire.

JESUS WASHES HIS DISCIPLES' FEET

13 *It was just before the Passover Feast. Jesus knew that the time had come for him to leave this world and go to the Father. Having loved his own who were in the world, he now showed them the full extent of his love.*

²The evening meal was being served, and the devil had already prompted Judas Iscariot, son of Simon, to betray Jesus. ³Jesus knew that the Father had put all things under his power, and that he had come from God and was returning to God; ⁴so he got up from the meal, took off his outer clothing, and wrapped a towel around his waist. ⁵After that, he poured water into a basin and began to wash his disciples' feet, drying them with the towel that was wrapped around him. ...

¹²When he had finished washing their feet, he put on his clothes and returned to his place. "Do you understand what I have done for you?" he asked them. ¹³"You call me 'Teacher' and 'Lord,' and rightly so, for that is what I am. ¹⁴Now that I, your Lord and Teacher, have washed your feet, you also should wash one another's feet. ¹⁵I have set you an example that you should do as I have done for you."

John 13:1–5,12–15

1. What is your first impression of this story about footwashing?
   ❏ This is confusing.
   ❏ This is gross.
   ❏ This is embarrassing.
   ❏ This is moving.
   ❏ This is irrelevant for our culture.
   ❏ This is a model for any culture.

2. What would you have done if you had been there and Jesus started to wash your feet?

- ❏ left the room
- ❏ refused to let him
- ❏ broken down and cried
- ❏ felt honored by his caring act
- ❏ just sat there—feeling guilty
- ❏ jumped up and tried to wash *his* feet

3. When you were in the seventh grade, what kind of servant-tasks were you expected to do around the house?

- ❏ make my bed
- ❏ clean my room
- ❏ take out the trash
- ❏ wash the dishes
- ❏ look after my sibling(s)
- ❏ do yard work
- ❏ help with cooking
- ❏ do laundry
- ❏ dust and vacuum
- ❏ all of the above
- ❏ none of the above

4. How did you feel about doing those tasks? What ingenious ways did you come up with to avoid them?

5. What's the lowliest or most disgusting chore you have to do at home or work now? How's your attitude toward it?

6. Who is one person in your life who has demonstrated what it means to "wash feet"? What did that person do for you?

7. What is the closest you have come to being part of a Christian community where you genuinely cared for one another and showed it?
   ❏ a music or drama group
   ❏ a sports team
   ❏ a youth group / small group
   ❏ my family
   ❏ a mission trip I went on
   ❏ a church
   ❏ the "gang" I used to run around with
   ❏ a group of people I got to know at a retreat or camp
   ❏ I'm not sure I have experienced this.
   ❏ other:_____

8. If your pastor went around and washed feet—including your feet—how would you feel?
   ❏ embarrassed   ❏ nervous
   ❏ really touched   ❏ confused

9. If Jesus came to you and wanted to care for you in a personal way right now, what would he probably do?
   ❏ I can't imagine.
   ❏ He would probably wash my feet.
   ❏ He might give me a hug.
   ❏ He would take me to a ball game—to get away from it all.
   ❏ He would be a friend and let me talk about my problems.
   ❏ He would take away my problems.
   ❏ other:_____

10. What's holding you back from living a life of service like Jesus demonstrated and taught?
    ❏ I'm afraid I'll be taken advantage of.
    ❏ I don't have time.
    ❏ I guess I'm too selfish.
    ❏ I haven't had many good role models.
    ❏ Nothing really—I'm doing my best.

11. What one thing will you do at home, work, school or church this week to follow Jesus' example of caring through serving?

12. How can the group pray for you?

CARING

FRIENDLY FIRE

Introduction

Even among the closest of friends, sometimes we hurt each other. In this Bible story, the apostle Peter asks Jesus what to do when you get hurt by a friend. He was probably talking about relationships within the close circle of friends who were followers of Christ.

Have someone read the story. Then, divide into groups of 4 and discuss the questionnaire. Remember, there are no right answers ... so feel free to share.

THE PARABLE OF THE UNMERCIFUL SERVANT

²¹ Then Peter came to Jesus and asked, "Lord, how many times shall I forgive my brother when he sins against me? Up to seven times?"

²² Jesus answered, "I tell you, not seven times, but seventy-seven times.

²³ "Therefore, the kingdom of heaven is like a king who wanted to settle accounts with his servants. ²⁴ As he began the settlement, a man who owed him ten thousand talents was brought to him. ²⁵ Since he was not able to pay, the master ordered that he and his wife and his children and all that he had be sold to repay the debt.

²⁶ "The servant fell on his knees before him. 'Be patient with me,' he begged, 'and I will pay back everything.' ²⁷ The servant's master took pity on him, canceled the debt and let him go.

²⁸ "But when that servant went out, he found one of his fellow servants who owed him a hundred denarii. He grabbed him and began to choke him. 'Pay back what you owe me!' he demanded.

²⁹ "His fellow servant fell to his knees and begged him, 'Be patient with me, and I will pay you back.'

³⁰ "But he refused. Instead, he went off and had the man thrown into prison until he could pay the debt. ³¹ When the other servants saw what had happened, they were greatly distressed and went and told their master everything that had happened.

³² "Then the master called the servant in. 'You wicked servant,' he said, 'I canceled all that debt of yours because you begged me to. ³³ Shouldn't you have had mercy on your fellow servant just as I had on you?' ³⁴ In anger his master turned him over to the jailers to be tortured, until he should pay back all he owed.

³⁵ "This is how my heavenly Father will treat each of you unless you forgive your brother from your heart."

Matthew 18:21–35

1. If you were Peter, what would have been your thoughts after Jesus answered your question?
   - ❏ I don't understand.
   - ❏ This is serious stuff.
   - ❏ This is going to be hard for me to do.
   - ❏ I'm anxious to give this a try.
   - ❏ I'm sorry I asked.

2. What was one of the worst things your brother or sister ever did to you?

3. To whom do you have to say "I'm sorry" the most?
   - ❏ my spouse / boyfriend / girlfriend
   - ❏ my parent(s)
   - ❏ my children
   - ❏ my brother / sister
   - ❏ another family member
   - ❏ a friend
   - ❏ my boss
   - ❏ a coworker
   - ❏ other:_____

4. Do you tend to be more like the master who forgave (v. 27) or the servant who wouldn't forgive (v. 30)?

5. Word gets back to you that something you shared in confidence with your youth group or small group last week is "all over town." What do you do?
   - ❏ stop going to the group
   - ❏ confront the group and tell them how this hurt me
   - ❏ never share anything again at the meetings
   - ❏ go to the leaders and ask them to handle it
   - ❏ go to the person I think said it and confront him or her
   - ❏ accept this as part of life and try to get on with it

6. When you get hurt in relationships, what do you usually do?
- ❐ have it out with the person
- ❐ sulk for three days
- ❐ withdraw into myself
- ❐ cry on someone's shoulder
- ❐ try to look at it from the other person's point of view
- ❐ watch reruns all night
- ❐ complain to God
- ❐ other:_____

7. What have you found helpful in dealing with conflict?
- ❐ writing out my feelings
- ❐ breaking off the relationship
- ❐ being up front with the person
- ❐ doing something nice for the person
- ❐ ignoring it and hoping it goes away
- ❐ appreciating God's forgiveness of me
- ❐ asking someone else to help deal with it
- ❐ seeing the other person as hurting himself or herself

8. What is hardest for you?
- ❐ forgiving again and again
- ❐ not punishing those who hurt me
- ❐ forgiving from my heart—I can say the words but I don't feel them.
- ❐ wondering how I can forgive without encouraging irresponsibility

9. Is there someone you need to forgive? If so, what is keeping you from forgiving them?

10. How would you like the group to pray for you?

CARING

SHARING YOUR FAITH

Introduction

How do you share your faith? What is witnessing? Witnessing is one beggar telling another beggar where to find food. This is an old definition, but it illustrates the Bible story that you are going to study.

This story takes place shortly after Jesus ascended to heaven and the Holy Spirit was poured out on the believers on the Day of Pentecost. At the gate to the temple in Jerusalem, a beggar approaches the apostles Peter and John for a hand-out. Listen to the story. Try to imagine yourself in this situation. Then move into groups of 4 and discuss the questionnaire.

PETER HEALS THE CRIPPLED BEGGAR

3 *One day Peter and John were going up to the temple at the time of prayer—at three in the afternoon. ²Now a man crippled from birth was being carried to the temple gate called Beautiful, where he was put every day to beg from those going into the temple courts. ³When he saw Peter and John about to enter, he asked them for money. ⁴Peter looked straight at him, as did John. Then Peter said, "Look at us!" ⁵So the man gave them his attention, expecting to get something from them.*

⁶Then Peter said, "Silver or gold I do not have, but what I have I give you. In the name of Jesus Christ of Nazareth, walk." ⁷Taking him by the right hand, he helped him up, and instantly the man's feet and ankles became strong. ⁸He jumped to his feet and began to walk. Then he went with them into the temple courts, walking and jumping, and praising God. ⁹When all the people saw him walking and praising God, ¹⁰they recognized him as the same man who used to sit begging at the temple gate called Beautiful, and they were filled with wonder and amazement at what had happened to him.

¹¹While the beggar held on to Peter and John, all the people were astonished and came running to them in the place called Solomon's Colonnade. ¹²When Peter saw this, he said to them: "Men of Israel, why does this surprise you? Why do you stare at us as if by our own power or godliness we had made this man walk? ¹³The God of Abraham, Isaac and Jacob, the God of our fathers, has glorified his servant Jesus. You handed him over to be killed, and you disowned him before Pilate, though he had decided to let him go. ¹⁴You disowned the Holy and Righteous One and asked that a murderer be released to you. ¹⁵You killed the author of life, but God raised him from the dead. We are witnesses of this. ¹⁶By faith in the name of Jesus, this man whom you see and know was made strong. It is Jesus' name and the faith that comes through him that has given this complete healing to him, as you can all see."

Acts 3:1–16

1. Had you been a reporter for *The Jerusalem Herald* and you were to write an article on this event, which of the following headlines would you have been most likely to have given it?
   - ❐ "Beggar Gets More Than He Asks For"
   - ❐ "Faith Healers Amaze Temple Crowd"
   - ❐ "Cripple Walks for First Time in His Life"
   - ❐ "Welfare Rolls Reduced by One"

2. How do you feel when you see someone begging on the street?
   - ❐ compassionate
   - ❐ embarrassed
   - ❐ I have really mixed feelings.
   - ❐ disgusted

3. If you were Peter, what would you have done when the beggar asked you for money?
   - ❐ the same thing Peter did
   - ❐ quickly walked by
   - ❐ asked John for a dime

4. When you have reached out to Jesus in the past, what motivated you to do so?
   - ❐ fear—of the judgment day
   - ❐ guilt—my conscience
   - ❐ heritage—the faith of my family
   - ❐ despair—I was burned out.
   - ❐ logic—I was convinced.
   - ❐ other:_____

5. Peter and John shared what they had with this beggar. What do you have that you can share with others?
   - ❐ maybe my lunch—that's about it
   - ❐ my ability to listen to their problems
   - ❐ my empathy with people who are hurting
   - ❐ my knowledge of the Bible
   - ❐ my faith in God and how it has helped me
   - ❐ my smiles and hugs
   - ❐ other:_____

6. Who do you admire, particularly in your school or workplace, for the way they share their faith?

7. If someone asked you, "Why do you go to church?" how would you answer?

8. What have you found to be the best way for you to share your faith?
   ❐ just being a friend
   ❐ giving the facts of the Gospel
   ❐ telling my own story of how I met Jesus
   ❐ living my life as a good example
   ❐ inviting a person to go to church or another event
   ❐ other:_____

9. What is your favorite excuse for *not* sharing the Good News of Christ?
   ❐ claiming I don't know enough
   ❐ saying I don't have time
   ❐ being too concerned with my own life
   ❐ thinking others can do it
   ❐ just ignoring it
   ❐ other:_____

10. Who is someone that you would like to share the Good News of Christ with?

11. What area of your life is "crippled" and in need of Christ's healing?

CARING

I APPRECIATE YOU

Introduction

This Scripture is taken from a longer passage about the kingdom of God. Jesus had been teaching his disciples about when the kingdom would come and who would be invited. He ends with this passage about "the sheep and the goats."

Listen to the passage. Then move into groups of 4 and discuss the questionnaire.

THE SHEEP AND THE GOATS

31"When the Son of Man comes in his glory, and all the angels with him, he will sit on his throne in heavenly glory. 32All the nations will be gathered before him, and he will separate the people one from another as a shepherd separates the sheep from the goats. 33He will put the sheep on his right and the goats on his left.

34"Then the King will say to those on his right, 'Come, you who are blessed by my Father; take your inheritance, the kingdom prepared for you since the creation of the world. 35For I was hungry and you gave me something to eat, I was thirsty and you gave me something to drink, I was a stranger and you invited me in, 36I needed clothes and you clothed me, I was sick and you looked after me, I was in prison and you came to visit me.'

37"Then the righteous will answer him, 'Lord, when did we see you hungry and feed you, or thirsty and give you something to drink? 38When did we see you a stranger and invite you in, or needing clothes and clothe you? 39When did we see you sick or in prison and go to visit you?'

40"The King will reply, 'I tell you the truth, whatever you did for one of the least of these brothers of mine, you did for me.'

41"Then he will say to those on his left, 'Depart from me, you who are cursed, into the eternal fire prepared for the devil and his angels. 42For I was hungry and you gave me nothing to eat, I was thirsty and you gave me nothing to drink, 43I was a stranger and you did not invite me in, I needed clothes and you did not clothe me, I was sick and in prison and you did not look after me.'

44"They also will answer, 'Lord, when did we see you hungry or thirsty or a stranger or needing clothes or sick or in prison, and did not help you?'

45"He will reply, 'I tell you the truth, whatever you did not do for one of the least of these, you did not do for me.'

46"Then they will go away to eternal punishment, but the righteous to eternal life."

Matthew 25:31–46

1. What little prize from the past have you kept because it was special to you?

2. Thinking about this parable Jesus told, how would you feel if you were placed in the group of sheep?
   - ❐ surprised
   - ❐ overjoyed
   - ❐ unworthy
   - ❐ grateful
   - ❐ relieved

3. How would you feel if you were placed in the group of goats?
   - ❐ surprised
   - ❐ terrified
   - ❐ angry
   - ❐ guilty

4. What person has always been there for you when you needed them?
   - ❐ my mother
   - ❐ another family member
   - ❐ my father
   - ❐ a close friend
   - ❐ both of my parents
   - ❐ a neighbor
   - ❐ my brother / sister
   - ❐ no one
   - ❐ a grandparent
   - ❐ other:_____

5. What kind of people do you have the most compassion for?
   - ❐ homeless
   - ❐ starving
   - ❐ lonely
   - ❐ refugees
   - ❐ sick or disabled
   - ❐ elderly
   - ❐ prisoners
   - ❐ other:_____

6. When was the last time you did something for someone hungry, alone, poor, sick or imprisoned?

7. If Jesus were to come today and evaluate your life, what would he say about how you have "looked after" him by caring for others?
   - ❐ "You're doing great!"
   - ❐ "You're doing a lot better than you used to."
   - ❐ "You used to do much better."
   - ❐ "You're doing the best you can."
   - ❐ "You're in big trouble!"

8. How would you rate this group on taking care of each other when someone is hurting or in need?
   ❐ I think we do a pretty good job.
   ❐ We are learning.
   ❐ We have a long way to go.
   ❐ We don't talk about these things.
   ❐ We really don't have any needs.

9. Think of this group as a community of love in which all of you are hurting in some way, and all of you are ministers in some way. Who would you nominate for special recognition for the following gifts of caring? Read the first category and let everyone nominate someone.

   _____*I was hungry and you gave me something to eat:* Your sharing of yourself in this group has caused me to grow.

   _____*I was thirsty and you gave me something to drink:* Your spiritual life and devotion to God has helped me find spiritual refreshment.

   _____*I was a stranger and you invited me in:* Your welcome when I came made me feel at home.

   _____*I needed clothes and you clothed me:* Your caring when I felt vulnerable and alone made me feel that somebody understands me.

   _____*I was sick and you looked after me:* Your reaching out to me when I was really down caused me to feel better and whole again.

10. What is one need you would like the group to pray about?

VALUES

PRIORITIES

Introduction

Stop the camera. If a soil inspector came today to inspect the soils in your life, what would they find? Jesus used this parable to explain why some people show the results of a healthy, balanced spiritual life and some do not. In this Bible study, you will have a chance to check your priorities and see if you can improve them.

Now, listen to the parable. Then, move into groups of 4 to share your responses.

THE PARABLE OF THE SOWER

⁴While a large crowd was gathering and people were coming to Jesus from town after town, he told this parable: ⁵"A farmer went out to sow his seed. As he was scattering the seed, some fell along the path; it was trampled on, and the birds of the air ate it up. ⁶Some fell on rock, and when it came up, the plants withered because they had no moisture. ⁷Other seed fell among thorns, which grew up with it and choked the plants. ⁸Still other seed fell on good soil. It came up and yielded a crop, a hundred times more than was sown."

When he said this, he called out, "He who has ears to hear, let him hear." ...

¹¹"This is the meaning of the parable: The seed is the word of God. ¹²Those along the path are the ones who hear, and then the devil comes and takes away the word from their hearts, so that they may not believe and be saved. ¹³Those on the rock are the ones who receive the word with joy when they hear it, but they have no root. They believe for a while, but in the time of testing they fall away. ¹⁴The seed that fell among thorns stands for those who hear, but as they go on their way they are choked by life's worries, riches and pleasures, and they do not mature. ¹⁵But the seed on good soil stands for those with a noble and good heart, who hear the word, retain it, and by persevering produce a crop.

Luke 8:4–8,11–15

1. As you listened to the description of the four soils in the Scripture, what was your first impression?
   ❐ This sounds like an article from *Better Homes and Gardens.*
   ❐ Oh no, this is going to be a boring Bible study.
   ❐ What is Jesus trying to say?
   ❐ I wonder which soil I am.

2. Who is the "green thumb" in your family? How are you at making things grow?

3. How are you at finishing what you start?

4. In the period of your life when your spiritual life was the most unfruitful, what was the main reason?
- ❐ I had a whole lot of problems.
- ❐ I didn't know about Christ.
- ❐ I knew about Christ, but my priorities were messed up.
- ❐ I lacked a supportive Christian community.
- ❐ I was living life *my* way.

5. What was the main factor at the time your life produced the best crop?
- ❐ I continually sought God's will.
- ❐ I had my priorities in order.
- ❐ I had few distractions in my life.
- ❐ I had a supportive Christian community.
- ❐ I had a strong devotional life.

6. What do you have in your life now that gives "depth to your soil" and nurtures your growth? (Choose as many as apply, and put a star by the one that is most important to you.)
- ❐ Christian parents / spouse
- ❐ other Christian relatives
- ❐ group Bible study
- ❐ personal devotions
- ❐ Christian friends
- ❐ Christian music
- ❐ regular worship
- ❐ some books I've read
- ❐ church activities
- ❐ other:_____

7. What are the "thorns" and "rocks" in your life which tend to choke out your spiritual growth? (Choose as many as apply.)
- ❏ pressure from friends or family
- ❏ influence of TV / movies / music
- ❏ concern about money
- ❏ lack of commitment or discipline
- ❏ a "rocky" home life
- ❏ suffering that makes it hard to believe in a good God
- ❏ desire for material things
- ❏ sexual temptations
- ❏ parties / alcohol / drugs
- ❏ worry about the future

8. How would you describe the root system of your spiritual life right now?
- ❏ pretty shallow
- ❏ growing
- ❏ strong and deep
- ❏ really dry

9. How often do you make hearing and acting on God's Word a priority in your life?
- ❏ all of the time
- ❏ most of the time
- ❏ some of the time
- ❏ Sorry you asked!

10. What specific "thorn of worry" would you like the group to pray with you about?

VALUES

POSSESSIONS

Introduction

The following parable shows us the effects of greed. Jesus calls us to share our resources with others for the sake of God's kingdom.

Listen to the parable. Then, move into groups of 4 and discuss the questionnaire below.

THE PARABLE OF THE RICH FOOL

[13]Someone in the crowd said to him, "Teacher, tell my brother to divide the inheritance with me."

[14]Jesus replied, "Man, who appointed me a judge or an arbiter between you?" [15]Then he said to them, "Watch out! Be on your guard against all kinds of greed; a man's life does not consist in the abundance of his possessions."

[16]And he told them this parable: "The ground of a certain rich man produced a good crop. [17]He thought to himself, 'What shall I do? I have no place to store my crops.'

[18]"Then he said, 'This is what I'll do. I will tear down my barns and build bigger ones, and there I will store all my grain and my goods. [19]And I'll say to myself, "You have plenty of good things laid up for many years. Take life easy; eat, drink and be merry."'

[20]"But God said to him, 'You fool! This very night your life will be demanded from you. Then who will get what you have prepared for yourself?'

[21]"This is how it will be with anyone who stores up things for himself but is not rich toward God."

Luke 12:13–21

1. Just for fun, if the Rich Fool in the parable (you can call him George Megabucks) lived in your community, what neighborhood would he live in and what kind of car would he drive?

2. Where would Mr. Megabucks go to church? How regular would he be in attendance?

3. How would you describe George?
- ☐ clever
- ☐ content
- ☐ secure
- ☐ materialistic
- ☐ a show-off
- ☐ screwed up
- ☐ immature
- ☐ brilliant
- ☐ unhappy
- ☐ dumb
- ☐ selfish
- ☐ lucky

4. After dying, how would the local paper describe George in the obituaries?
- ☐ a tireless worker
- ☐ a success story
- ☐ foolish
- ☐ enterprising

5. If you had been a friend of the rich man in this parable, how would you have acted toward him?
- ☐ kissed up to him so he would invite me to his parties
- ☐ snubbed him just to show everyone I don't care about money
- ☐ treated him like everyone else
- ☐ witnessed to him about Christ
- ☐ shown him how to relax and just enjoy life

6. If you suddenly came into money, what would you do with it?
- ☐ quit school or work—travel the world
- ☐ share it with friends or family
- ☐ buy a car or motorcycle
- ☐ throw a huge party
- ☐ not let anyone know
- ☐ give it to the needy
- ☐ keep doing the things I am doing now
- ☐ other:_____

7. What do you value most in life? (Rank your top three choices.)

___ my family

___ my friends

___ my assets

___ my good health

___ my work

___ my faith

___ my integrity

___ my memories

___ my time

8. If you should die today, what would the people closest to you say about you in the newspaper? Finish the sentences below with the first thing that comes to mind. If the others in your group want to help you with your answers, let them speak up.

❐ Last night (fill in your name) died suddenly.

❐ He / She will always be remembered at church for their ...

❐ He / She always had time for ...

❐ He / She felt that possessions were ...

❐ He / She treated people like ...

❐ On his / her tombstone, the following words are inscribed:

9. If you were to give a "weather report" on your life recently, what would it be?

❐ dark and stormy

❐ bright and sunny

❐ partly cloudy

❐ dreary and gray

❐ other: _____

10. In light of the "weather" in your life, how would you like the group to pray for you this week?

VALUES

RESPONSIBILITY

Introduction

In this Bible study, you are going to study the parable of the talents. (A talent was a unit of coins worth more than a thousand dollars.) We will look at a man who didn't use the money he was given. Jesus calls this man wicked and lazy. The present-day use of "talent" as an ability comes from this parable. As you listen to the parable, think about what Jesus might say to you about taking responsibility for your time, money and abilities.

Listen to the passage. Then move into groups of 4 and discuss the questionnaire below.

THE PARABLE OF THE TALENTS

14 "Again, it will be like a man going on a journey, who called his servants and entrusted his property to them. 15To one he gave five talents of money, to another two talents, and to another one talent, each according to his ability. Then he went on his journey. 16The man who had received the five talents went at once and put his money to work and gained five more. 17So also, the one with the two talents gained two more. 18But the man who had received the one talent went off, dug a hole in the ground and hid his master's money.

19 "After a long time the master of those servants returned and settled accounts with them. 20The man who had received the five talents brought the other five. 'Master,' he said, 'you entrusted me with five talents. See, I have gained five more.'

21 "His master replied, 'Well done, good and faithful servant! You have been faithful with a few things; I will put you in charge of many things. Come and share your master's happiness!'

22 "The man with the two talents also came. 'Master,' he said, 'you entrusted me with two talents; see, I have gained two more.'

23 "His master replied, 'Well done, good and faithful servant! You have been faithful with a few things; I will put you in charge of many things. Come and share your master's happiness!'

24 "Then the man who had received the one talent came. 'Master,' he said, 'I knew that you are a hard man, harvesting where you have not sown and gathering where you have not scattered seed. 25So I was afraid and went out and hid your talent in the ground. See, here is what belongs to you.'

26 "His master replied, 'You wicked, lazy servant! So you knew that I harvest where I have not sown and gather where I have not scattered seed? 27Well then, you should have put my money on deposit with the bankers, so that when I returned I would have received it back with interest.

28 " 'Take the talent from him and give it to the one who has the ten talents. 29For everyone who has will be given more, and he will have an abundance. Whoever does not have, even what he has will be taken from him. [30]And throw that worthless servant outside, into the darkness, where there will be weeping and gnashing of teeth.' "

Matthew 25:14–30

1. What would the *Wall Street Journal* call the way the master in the parable treated his servants?
   ❐ shrewd
   ❐ fair
   ❐ businesslike
   ❐ unfair

2. Are you more of a saver or a spender?

3. Which of the three servants in this parable can you relate to most easily?
   ❐ the one who was given five talents—I've been greatly blessed.
   ❐ the one who was given two talents—I've done okay with what I've had to work with.
   ❐ the one who was given one talent—I always get the short end!

4. How do you feel when you are given a lot of responsibility?
   ❐ nervous—I hope I don't blow it!
   ❐ proud—People believe in me!
   ❐ overwhelmed—I can't handle it!
   ❐ confident—I can handle it!

5. Write three talents you have discovered or which others have said you have. Then assign each talent a number (from the scale below) according to how well you're using that talent right now:

   1   2   3   4   5   6   7   8   9   10
   burying it   **fully invested**

   talent #1:_____   usage:_____
   talent #2:_____   usage:_____
   talent #3:_____   usage:_____

6. What motivates you to use your time, resources and abilities for God's kingdom?
   - ❐ fear of the Master
   - ❐ people's appreciation
   - ❐ God's approval
   - ❐ a chance for greater responsibility
   - ❐ fellowship with the Master
   - ❐ rewards in the next life
   - ❐ other:_____

7. Which of the following statements best describes how you feel about the way you are "investing" your life?
   - ❐ I'm quite satisfied.
   - ❐ I would like to make some changes.
   - ❐ I'm not sure what it means to invest my life.
   - ❐ I'm not being very responsible in this area.
   - ❐ I feel like I'm on hold.

8. What are your goals for the future? What are you doing now to get you there?

9. What do you need to do to be a more responsible "servant"?
   - ❐ have more confidence I can do what is asked of me
   - ❐ become more aware of my strengths and abilities
   - ❐ take my responsibilities more seriously
   - ❐ trust in God to help me
   - ❐ get more encouragement from others
   - ❐ Responsible?—I just want to have fun!

10. If the Master returned today, how well would he say you have been using what he gave you?

11. Name one thing you can do this week to prepare for Christ's coming. How can the group support you in prayer?

MORALITY

Introduction

Try to imagine the picture of a giant banquet hall where King Herod is sitting at a drunken feast. Herodias, his wife, is sitting next to him. (Herodias left Herod's brother to marry Herod.) Off in prison is John the Baptist, who dared to tell the king that it was wrong to marry his brother's wife. Herod faces a moral dilemma after his stepdaughter (whose name was Salome) performs what was surely a highly sensual dance.

Listen to the story as it develops. Then, move into groups of 4 and discuss the questionnaire below.

JOHN THE BAPTIST BEHEADED

[14]King Herod heard about this, for Jesus' name had become well known. Some were saying, "John the Baptist has been raised from the dead, and that is why miraculous powers are at work in him."

[15]Others said, "He is Elijah."

And still others claimed, "He is a prophet, like one of the prophets of long ago."

[16]But when Herod heard this, he said, "John, the man I beheaded, has been raised from the dead!"

[17]For Herod himself had given orders to have John arrested, and he had him bound and put in prison. He did this because of Herodias, his brother Philip's wife, whom he had married. [18]For John had been saying to Herod, "It is not lawful for you to have your brother's wife." [19]So Herodias nursed a grudge against John and wanted to kill him. But she was not able to, [20]because Herod feared John and protected him, knowing him to be a righteous and holy man. When Herod heard John, he was greatly puzzled; yet he liked to listen to him.

[21]Finally the opportune time came. On his birthday Herod gave a banquet for his high officials and military commanders and the leading men of Galilee. [22]When the daughter of Herodias came in and danced, she pleased Herod and his dinner guests.

The king said to the girl, "Ask me for anything you want, and I'll give it to you." [23]And he promised her with an oath, "Whatever you ask I will give you, up to half my kingdom."

[24]She went out and said to her mother, "What shall I ask for?"

"The head of John the Baptist," she answered.

[25]At once the girl hurried in to the king with the request: "I want you to give me right now the head of John the Baptist on a platter."

[26]The king was greatly distressed, but because of his oaths and his dinner guests, he did not want to refuse her. [27]So he immediately sent an executioner with orders to bring John's head. The man went, beheaded John in the prison, [28]and brought back his head on a platter. He presented it to the girl, and she gave it to her mother. [29]On hearing of this, John's disciples came and took his body and laid it in a tomb.

Mark 6:14–29

1. If tabloids existed back then, what would the headlines be?
   - ❐ "Prophet Loses Head Over Girl"
   - ❐ "First Lady in Charge at Palace"
   - ❐ "Popular Preacher Pays the Price for Exotic Dancer"
   - ❐ "Royal Birthday Party Gets Out of Hand"
   - ❐ "John the Baptist Returns From the Dead to Haunt Herod"

2. What rating would you give this story?
   - ❐ G
   - ❐ PG
   - ❐ PG-13
   - ❐ R
   - ❐ X

3. Of the three people involved in the death of John the Baptist, which one do you feel the greatest anger toward because of their moral corruption?
   - ❐ King Herod—because he took his brother's wife and gave the order to kill the person who spoke out against him
   - ❐ Herodias—because she deserted her husband and tricked the king into killing John the Baptist out of spite
   - ❐ Herodias' daughter—because she let her mother use her "dirty dancing" to have John the Baptist killed

4. John the Baptist dared to tell the king that it was wrong to take his brother's wife. If you were John the Baptist, what would you have done?
   - ❐ just what he did
   - ❐ kept my mouth shut
   - ❐ written an anonymous letter to the editor
   - ❐ said my peace and then ran for the hills

5. In your own circles, who do you admire for they way they have stood up for what is right?

6. What is the closest you have come to "losing your head" for something you said or believed in?

7. When you have to make a moral decision, what do you do?
   - ❏ struggle for days
   - ❏ make a snap decision
   - ❏ hope it will go away
   - ❏ go for a long walk
   - ❏ ask for help
   - ❏ see what my friends or family are doing
   - ❏ other:_____

8. Specifically, where do you draw the line when it comes to entertainment with sexual or violent content?

9. How would you rate yourself in standing up for what is right? Finish the sentence below by choosing one in each category:

IN STANDING UP FOR WHAT I THINK IS RIGHT, I (AM) ...

Rock of Gibraltar _____Jello pudding

stick to my convictions _____waver back and forth

usually follow the crowd _____rely on my own judgment

10. What is your biggest fear in standing up for what you believe?
    - ❏ that I will be laughed at
    - ❏ that I will be alone
    - ❏ that I will lose my friends
    - ❏ that I will look stupid

11. How can the group pray for you, particularly in relation to moral issues?

BOTTOM LINE

Introduction

This Bible study looks at a parable that Jesus used at the close of the Sermon on the Mount to illustrate two different kinds of people.

Listen to the parable carefully, then move into groups of 4 and discuss the questionnaire.

THE WISE AND FOOLISH BUILDERS

[24] "Therefore everyone who hears these words of mine and puts them into practice is like a wise man who built his house on the rock. [25] The rain came down, the streams rose, and the winds blew and beat against that house; yet it did not fall, because it had its foundation on the rock. [26] But everyone who hears these words of mine and does not put them into practice is like a foolish man who built his house on sand. [27] The rain came down, the streams rose, and the winds blew and beat against that house, and it fell with a great crash."

Matthew 7:24–27

1. If you could build your dream house, where would you build it and what would it be like?

2. What is the worst storm you can remember?

3. Who (other than God) is the "Rock of Gibraltar" in your life? What is it about that person that makes them so stable?

4. In this parable, what exactly is Jesus promising to someone who is willing to live by his words?
   - ❏ that you will never experience storms
   - ❏ that you will experience the same storms as everybody else
   - ❏ that the storms will not destroy your faith
   - ❏ that you will get a new house if your old one collapses

5. If you could compare your life to a house, and every room in your house to a living space in your life, what would a building inspector say?

Let one person in your group read the description of one room below. Then, let everyone in your group call out a number from 1 to 10—1 being SHAKY and 10 being ROCK SOLID. Then, go on to the next room and let everyone call out a number for this room.

LIVING ROOM: I have my life in order; I know what I want to do; my values are well-defined; my moral principles are clear; I am feeling good about myself and my lifestyle right now.

1	2	3	4	5	6	7	8	9	10

RECREATION ROOM: I have a healthy balance in my schedule for leisure; I use my spare time carefully—to restore my mind and spirit as well as my body; I am feeling good about my priorities and the way I use my time.

1	2	3	4	5	6	7	8	9	10

FAMILY ROOM: I have a good relationship with my family; we have learned to talk about our differences; we deal with our conflicts; we build up one another during "stormy" times; I am feeling good about my family and enjoy being with them.

1	2	3	4	5	6	7	8	9	10

LIBRARY: I feed my mind in wholesome, appropriate and balanced ways; I make decisions based on definite values and moral principles, and don't just cave in to the pressures of the world.

1	2	3	4	5	6	7	8	9	10

PHYSICAL FITNESS ROOM: I try to keep in shape and maintain a healthy lifestyle; I can sleep nights and weather the "storms" of life without getting fatigued and depressed.

1	2	3	4	5	6	7	8	9	10

GUEST ROOM: I have a good relationship with my friends; I enjoy being with people without feeling dependent upon them; I can belong to the crowd without accepting or bowing to their values; I can stand against social pressure to conform, yet am sensitive to open the door when someone needs a little warmth.

| 1 | 2 | 3 | 4 | 5 | 6 | 7 | 8 | 9 | 10 |

6. Being totally honest, what is the foundation you depend on?
   ❐ my abilities
   ❐ my status
   ❐ wishful thinking
   ❐ self-confidence
   ❐ good health
   ❐ other people
   ❐ my resources
   ❐ faith in Christ

7. If you could compare your spiritual foundation right now to a house, what would it be?
   ❐ shaky   ❐ solid
   ❐ brand new   ❐ temporary
   ❐ slipping   ❐ rebuilding

8. In the last year, would you say your spiritual formation has gotten weaker or stronger?

9. What "storm" are you facing now? How can the group pray for you right now and in the days ahead?

PRESSURES

STRESS

Introduction

In this Bible study you will take a look at a story of Jesus and his disciples in a storm—a big storm—that caused a lot of stress.

Now, listen to the Bible story. Then, quickly move into groups of 4 and discuss the questionnaire.

JESUS CALMS THE STORM

³⁵*That day when evening came, he said to his disciples, "Let us go over to the other side."* ³⁶*Leaving the crowd behind, they took him along, just as he was, in the boat. There were also other boats with him.* ³⁷*A furious squall came up, and the waves broke over the boat, so that it was nearly swamped.* ³⁸*Jesus was in the stern, sleeping on a cushion. The disciples woke him and said to him, "Teacher, don't you care if we drown?"*

³⁹*He got up, rebuked the wind and said to the waves, "Quiet! Be still!" Then the wind died down and it was completely calm.*

⁴⁰*He said to his disciples, "Why are you so afraid? Do you still have no faith?"*

⁴¹*They were terrified and asked each other, "Who is this? Even the wind and the waves obey him!"*

Mark 4:35–41

1. If you were a reporter assigned to the Lake of Galilee beat, what headline would you give this event?
   ❏ "Self-Proclaimed Messiah Proves Himself"
   ❏ "Religious Leader Gives Followers a Scare"
   ❏ "Prophet Demonstrates Sleeping Disorder"
   ❏ "Even Nature Obeys Miracle Worker"

2. If you had been one of the disciples when the boat was about to sink, what would you have done?
   ❏ jumped overboard
   ❏ screamed for help
   ❏ started bailing water
   ❏ taken command
   ❏ acted like nothing was wrong
   ❏ woken up Jesus

3. Who in your family is good at keeping calm in the storms of life? How do they do it?

4. What brings on most of the "storms" in your life?
   - ❏ pressures at work or school
   - ❏ family problems
   - ❏ financial difficulties
   - ❏ hassles with other relationships
   - ❏ health problems
   - ❏ overwhelming demands
   - ❏ insecurity: worry about the future
   - ❏ disappointment: feelings of failure
   - ❏ tragedy: grief and loss
   - ❏ other:_____

5. If you could have three wishes, which three would you choose from the list below?
   - ❏ win the lottery: never have to work again
   - ❏ secure job: lifetime guarantee with benefits
   - ❏ stress-free life: no struggles, no tension
   - ❏ close family: no hassles, lots of love and support
   - ❏ good health: long life full of vigor and vitality
   - ❏ one deep, abiding friendship: someone who will be close to me forever
   - ❏ happiness: a life full of joy and surprises
   - ❏ success: fame and recognition in my chosen field
   - ❏ direction: to know what I should do with my life
   - ❏ strong faith: a deep, satisfying relationship with God

6. What do you do when storms come up in your life?
   - ❏ turn to a person I can trust
   - ❏ withdraw into myself
   - ❏ turn to God
   - ❏ get touchy and irritable
   - ❏ take charge of things
   - ❏ act like nothing is wrong
   - ❏ panic

7. As time goes on, have you seen improvement in the way you handle storms? What difference does your faith in Christ make?

8. The disciples asked Jesus an interesting question—"Don't you care if we drown?" When was the last time you wondered if God cared about you?

9. If you could compare your own life to the storm in this story, where are you right now?
   - ❏ floating on smooth waters
   - ❏ seeing just a few storm clouds
   - ❏ sensing a storm is brewing
   - ❏ in the middle of the storm, bailing water like mad
   - ❏ sinking fast
   - ❏ seeing the storm winds die down and calm return

10. "Quiet! Be still!" If Jesus were to speak these words to you today, what would they mean?
    - ❏ Settle down.
    - ❏ Relax and let God handle this.
    - ❏ Shut up and listen.
    - ❏ Keep the faith.
    - ❏ Hang in there.
    - ❏ Turn the controls of your life over to God.
    - ❏ other:_____

11. What stress do you have that you need Jesus to calm? Pray for each other.

PRESSURES

WORRIES

Introduction

"Don't worry—be happy" the song says. If only it were that easy! Jesus had a lot to say about pressures like worry. This Bible study comes from a well-known Scripture about worry.

Listen to these words of Jesus as someone reads the passage. Then move into groups of 4 and discuss the questionnaire.

DO NOT WORRY

[24] *"No one can serve two masters. Either he will hate the one and love the other, or he will be devoted to the one and despise the other. You cannot serve both God and Money.*

[25] *"Therefore I tell you, do not worry about your life, what you will eat or drink; or about your body, what you will wear. Is not life more important than food, and the body more important than clothes? [26] Look at the birds of the air; they do not sow or reap or store away in barns, and yet your heavenly Father feeds them. Are you not much more valuable than they? [27] Who of you by worrying can add a single hour to his life?*

[28] *"And why do you worry about clothes? See how the lilies of the field grow. They do not labor or spin. [29] Yet I tell you that not even Solomon in all his splendor was dressed like one of these. [30] If that is how God clothes the grass of the field, which is here today and tomorrow is thrown into the fire, will he not much more clothe you, O you of little faith? [31] So do not worry, saying, 'What shall we eat?' or 'What shall we drink?' or 'What shall we wear?' [32] For the pagans run after all these things, and your heavenly Father knows that you need them. [33] But seek first his kingdom and his righteousness, and all these things will be given to you as well. [34] Therefore do not worry about tomorrow, for tomorrow will worry about itself. Each day has enough trouble of its own."*

Matthew 6:24–34

1. If Jesus lived today, how would he dress?
   - ❐ in jeans and a T-shirt
   - ❐ in a business suit
   - ❐ with thrift store donations
   - ❐ like a pastor or priest
   - ❐ like a fashion model—the latest fad
   - ❐ He wouldn't care what he wore.

2. What kind of car do you think Jesus would drive?
   - ❐ a fancy Mercedes
   - ❐ an old junker
   - ❐ a classic Corvette
   - ❐ a pickup truck
   - ❐ a minivan, to hold his disciples
   - ❐ a bus—to bring in the crowds
   - ❐ nothing—He would either walk or use public transportation.

3. When Jesus said, "Do not worry about tomorrow," what did he mean?
   - ❐ Don't plan ahead.
   - ❐ Plan ahead so you don't worry.
   - ❐ Worry is a waste of time and energy.
   - ❐ Live for today.
   - ❐ Trust God with things you can't control.

4. If you really followed the teaching of this passage, how would it change your behavior?
   - ❐ I wouldn't be caught up in material things.
   - ❐ I would spend more time helping people.
   - ❐ I would be less concerned about how I look and dress.
   - ❐ I would give more money to the poor.
   - ❐ I would make my spiritual life my highest priority.
   - ❐ I wouldn't worry so much.
   - ❐ I would spend more time with church activities.
   - ❐ other:_____

5. What is your favorite way of dealing with your problems? Pick your most and least frequent ways:
   - ❐ deny that I have any
   - ❐ talk to a close friend
   - ❐ worry a lot
   - ❐ eat a lot
   - ❐ ask for help
   - ❐ go for a walk
   - ❐ talk to God about them
   - ❐ get busy and try to forget them
   - ❐ accept problems as part of life
   - ❐ listen to music until I feel better
   - ❐ other:_____

6. If you could describe a good goal for dealing with the most difficult problem you are facing at the moment, what would it be?
   - ☐ learn to laugh more at my troubles
   - ☐ learn to live one day at a time
   - ☐ get out of the situation I'm in
   - ☐ lower the expectations I've placed on myself and others
   - ☐ focus more on God's kingdom and less on mine
   - ☐ simplify my lifestyle
   - ☐ take time to smell the flowers
   - ☐ other:_____

7. On a scale from 1 (low) to 10 (high), what is the stress level in your life at the moment?

8. If your doctor told you that you had to reduce the stress in your life, what would have to change?

9. What is the biggest worry you have about the coming week? How can this group pray for you regarding that concern?

PRESSURES

SHATTERED DREAMS

Introduction

In this Bible study, we want you to listen to the experience of two followers of Jesus who may have lost hope and decided to return home. It is right after the resurrection of Jesus, but these two followers are still sad and confused.

Listen in on their conversation as Jesus comes alongside of them and lets them talk about their disappointment and shattered dreams. Then, move quickly into groups of 4 and discuss the questionnaire.

ON THE ROAD TO EMMAUS

13Now that same day two of them were going to a village called Emmaus, about seven miles from Jerusalem. 14They were talking with each other about everything that had happened. 15As they talked and discussed these things with each other, Jesus himself came up and walked along with them; 16but they were kept from recognizing him.

17He asked them, "What are you discussing together as you walk along?"

They stood still, their faces downcast. 18One of them, named Cleopas, asked him, "Are you only a visitor to Jerusalem and do not know the things that have happened there in these days?"

19"What things?" he asked.

"About Jesus of Nazareth," they replied. "He was a prophet, powerful in word and deed before God and all the people. 20The chief priests and our rulers handed him over to be sentenced to death, and they crucified him; 21but we had hoped that he was the one who was going to redeem Israel. And what is more, it is the third day since all this took place. 22In addition, some of our women amazed us. They went to the tomb early this morning 23but didn't find his body. They came and told us that they had seen a vision of angels, who said he was alive. 24Then some of our companions went to the tomb and found it just as the women had said, but him they did not see."

25He said to them, "How foolish you are, and how slow of heart to believe all that the prophets have spoken! 26Did not the Christ have to suffer these things and then enter his glory?" 27And beginning with Moses and all the Prophets, he explained to them what was said in all the Scriptures concerning himself.

28As they approached the village to which they were going, Jesus acted as if he were going farther. 29But they urged him strongly, "Stay with us, for it is nearly evening; the day is almost over." So he went in to stay with them.

30When he was at the table with them, he took bread, gave thanks, broke it and began to give it to them. 31Then their eyes were opened and they recognized him, and he disappeared from their sight. 32They asked each other, "Were not our hearts burning within us while he talked with us on the road and opened the Scriptures to us?"

[33] They got up and returned at once to Jerusalem. There they found the Eleven and those with them, assembled together [34] and saying, "It is true! The Lord has risen and has appeared to Simon." [35] Then the two told what had happened on the way, and how Jesus was recognized by them when he broke the bread.

Luke 24:13–35

1. If you got some really bad news today, where would you go to get yourself together?

2. Why didn't the two disciples in this story recognize Jesus when he joined them?
   - ❑ They were preoccupied.
   - ❑ They were depressed.
   - ❑ They couldn't recognize Jesus in his resurrected body.
   - ❑ They refused to believe their eyes.
   - ❑ God kept them from recognizing him.

3. When did you last experience a broken dream or a broken heart?

4. What is the closest you have come to "throwing in the towel" and giving up on your relationship with God?

5. What was it that brought you back to faith?

6. What did you learn during that time you were away from God?
   - ❑ It's lonely out there.
   - ❑ God never leaves you alone.
   - ❑ It's okay to struggle.
   - ❑ Once you've given your heart to God, God is going to be more visible.
   - ❑ There is always a way home.

7. What helps you recognize Jesus alongside you when you are down?
   - ❏ taking time to be alone with God
   - ❏ talking with someone who cares
   - ❏ reading Scripture
   - ❏ getting away from the situation
   - ❏ focusing on worship
   - ❏ fellowshipping with others
   - ❏ other:_____

8. What does the resurrected Jesus need to change in your life?
   - ❏ my spiritual vision
   - ❏ my unbelief
   - ❏ my discouragement
   - ❏ my loneliness
   - ❏ my disillusionment
   - ❏ other:_____

9. How would you describe your "walk" with Christ right now?
   - ❏ up and down
   - ❏ growing
   - ❏ very close
   - ❏ slipping
   - ❏ blah
   - ❏ exciting
   - ❏ other:_____

10. If Jesus showed up at your meeting today, what would he likely say to you personally? To your group?

11. How can the group pray for you?

PRESSURES

OLD HABITS

Introduction

This Bible story finds the apostle Peter in jail because of his faith and preaching. As you listen to the story, try to identify with Peter and with his fellow believers as they pray for him. Then think about what this story of Peter's miraculous escape has to say about the things that may hold you captive.

Read the Scripture passage now. Then, move into groups of 4 and discuss the questionnaire.

PETER'S MIRACULOUS ESCAPE FROM PRISON

12 *It was about this time that King Herod arrested some who belonged to the church, intending to persecute them. ²He had James, the brother of John, put to death with the sword. ³When he saw that this pleased the Jews, he proceeded to seize Peter also. This happened during the Feast of Unleavened Bread. ⁴After arresting him, he put him in prison, handing him over to be guarded by four squads of four soldiers each. Herod intended to bring him out for public trial after the Passover.*

⁵So Peter was kept in prison, but the church was earnestly praying to God for him.

⁶The night before Herod was to bring him to trial, Peter was sleeping between two soldiers, bound with two chains, and sentries stood guard at the entrance. ⁷Suddenly an angel of the Lord appeared and a light shone in the cell. He struck Peter on the side and woke him up. "Quick, get up!" he said, and the chains fell off Peter's wrists.

⁸Then the angel said to him, "Put on your clothes and sandals." And Peter did so. "Wrap your cloak around you and follow me," the angel told him. ⁹Peter followed him out of the prison, but he had no idea that what the angel was doing was really happening; he thought he was seeing a vision. ¹⁰They passed the first and second guards and came to the iron gate leading to the city. It opened for them by itself, and they went through it. When they had walked the length of one street, suddenly the angel left him.

¹¹Then Peter came to himself and said, "Now I know without a doubt that the Lord sent his angel and rescued me from Herod's clutches and from everything the Jewish people were anticipating."

¹²When this had dawned on him, he went to the house of Mary the mother of John, also called Mark, where many people had gathered and were praying. ¹³Peter knocked at the outer entrance, and a servant girl named Rhoda came to answer the door. ¹⁴When she recognized Peter's voice, she was so overjoyed she ran back without opening it and exclaimed, "Peter is at the door!"

¹⁵"You're out of your mind," they told her. When she kept insisting that it was so, they said, "It must be his angel."

¹⁶But Peter kept on knocking, and when they opened the door and saw him, they were astonished.

Acts 12:1–16

1. "The night before Herod was to bring him to trial, Peter was sleeping between two soldiers, bound with two chains, and sentries stood guard at the entrance. Suddenly an angel of the Lord appeared and a light shone in the cell. He struck Peter on the side and woke him up. 'Quick, get up!' he said, and the chains fell off Peter's wrists." Imagine you are Peter. What would you have said?
   - ❒ "Okay, okay—I'm getting up!"
   - ❒ "This must be a dream."
   - ❒ "This must be my guardian angel!"
   - ❒ "This isn't going to go over very well with the guards."
   - ❒ "Praise God! My prayers have been answered!"

2. Now imagine that you were at the prayer meeting when Rhoda announced (without opening the door) that "Peter is at the door!" What would you have said?
   - ❒ "You're out of your mind!"
   - ❒ "Well, let him in!"
   - ❒ "It must be Peter's guardian angel."
   - ❒ "Just as I expected!"
   - ❒ "Praise God! My prayers have been answered!"

3. When has God surprised you by intervening in an "imprisoning" situation that you thought was hopeless?

4. In your school or job, what is the most common addiction?
   - ❒ alcohol
   - ❒ food / weight control
   - ❒ exercise
   - ❒ spending / gambling
   - ❒ anger / violence
   - ❒ work / achievement
   - ❒ drugs
   - ❒ tobacco
   - ❒ TV / movies
   - ❒ sex / pornography
   - ❒ other:_____

5. From your experience, what could you share to help someone who feels they are helplessly addicted?

6. What kinds of things do you find to be most imprisoning?
   - ☐ habits / addictions
   - ☐ bad relationships
   - ☐ my desire for things
   - ☐ school / work
   - ☐ a stagnant spiritual life
   - ☐ my impulses
   - ☐ my fears
   - ☐ my friends' expectations
   - ☐ my parents' / spouse's expectations
   - ☐ a health problem / physical limitation
   - ☐ other:_____

7. What would most help you to find freedom from these things?
   - ☐ an angel coming from heaven to take care of it all
   - ☐ friends praying for me, and really believing it can happen
   - ☐ my own confidence in God's ability to help me
   - ☐ my own desire to change
   - ☐ So who wants to change—a prison is a secure place!

8. What can this group do to help you be free?
   - ☐ leave me alone
   - ☐ pray for me
   - ☐ let me know I'm okay
   - ☐ hold me accountable
   - ☐ call me to see how I'm doing
   - ☐ share some of their own struggles
   - ☐ help me to understand myself and to change
   - ☐ other:_____

9. If you, like Peter, were arrested by a repressive government for being a Christian, what evidence would there be that you are "guilty"? What evidence would there be that you are "innocent"?

10. What is God saying to you through this study? How can the group pray for you?

PRESSURES

SHAME AND BLAME

Introduction

As a prostitute, the woman in this Bible story felt a great deal of shame and blame. Yet she longed for God's forgiveness.

Listen to the story as it unfolds. Then, move into groups of 4 and discuss the questionnaire.

JESUS ANOINTED BY A SINFUL WOMAN

36Now one of the Pharisees invited Jesus to have dinner with him, so he went to the Pharisee's house and reclined at the table. 37When a woman who had lived a sinful life in that town learned that Jesus was eating at the Pharisee's house, she brought an alabaster jar of perfume, 38and as she stood behind him at his feet weeping, she began to wet his feet with her tears. Then she wiped them with her hair, kissed them and poured perfume on them.

39When the Pharisee who had invited him saw this, he said to himself, "If this man were a prophet, he would know who is touching him and what kind of woman she is—that she is a sinner."

40Jesus answered him, "Simon, I have something to tell you."

"Tell me, teacher," he said.

41"Two men owed money to a certain moneylender. One owed him five hundred denarii, and the other fifty. 42Neither of them had the money to pay him back, so he canceled the debts of both. Now which of them will love him more?"

43Simon replied, "I suppose the one who had the bigger debt canceled."

"You have judged correctly," Jesus said.

44Then he turned toward the woman and said to Simon, "Do you see this woman? I came into your house. You did not give me any water for my feet, but she wet my feet with her tears and wiped them with her hair. 45You did not give me a kiss, but this woman, from the time I entered, has not stopped kissing my feet. 46You did not put oil on my head, but she has poured perfume on my feet. 47Therefore, I tell you, her many sins have been forgiven—for she loved much. But he who has been forgiven little loves little."

48Then Jesus said to her, "Your sins are forgiven."

49The other guests began to say among themselves, "Who is this who even forgives sins?"

50Jesus said to the woman, "Your faith has saved you; go in peace."

Luke 7:36–50

1. What section would the local newspaper put this story in?
   - ❐ the society page—highlighting that a prostitute crashed the dinner this Pharisee had for Jesus
   - ❐ the gossip column—because of the scandalous way the prostitute acted toward Jesus
   - ❐ the religion page—headlining Jesus' claim that the prostitute's sins were forgiven
   - ❐ the business section—announcing the woman's departure from her profession

2. How would you have felt watching the woman anoint Jesus like she did in verse 38?
   - ❐ embarrassed
   - ❐ confused
   - ❐ moved
   - ❐ disgusted

3. How would your group react if this woman "crashed" your meeting?
   - ❐ We would accept her easily.
   - ❐ We would want to accept her, but it would be awkward.
   - ❐ We wouldn't accept her.
   - ❐ We would want to see some evidence of change.

4. When in your life have you most felt like an outsider who didn't belong?

5. Who in your life has played the role of Simon, questioning your value? Who has played the role of Jesus, believing in and sticking up for you?

6. Who do you identify with most in this story?
   - ❐ the woman—because I feel bad about my past
   - ❐ the Pharisee—because I have a tendency to be judgmental
   - ❐ Jesus—because hypocritical attitudes make me angry

7. What have you found to be the hardest thing about dealing with sin and failure?
   - ❐ admitting it to myself
   - ❐ admitting it to someone who can help me
   - ❐ receiving God's forgiveness
   - ❐ forgiving myself
   - ❐ facing the blame of others
   - ❐ facing my own feelings of shame
   - ❐ making amends
   - ❐ other:_____

8. What needs to happen for you to feel the kind of forgiveness this woman felt?
   - ❐ I need to take an honest look at my life.
   - ❐ I need to get my life straightened out first.
   - ❐ I need to find someone to talk to who is as sympathetic as Jesus.
   - ❐ I need to stop listening to the "Pharisees" who condemn me.
   - ❐ I need to accept the forgiveness which Jesus has already offered.
   - ❐ Nothing really, because I'm feeling Christ's forgiveness fully right now.
   - ❐ other:_____

9. Where in your life do you need to reach out and "touch" Jesus? Specifically, what do you need to receive from him?
   - ❐ forgiveness
   - ❐ spiritual healing
   - ❐ strength
   - ❐ relational healing
   - ❐ emotional healing
   - ❐ other:_____

10. How can this group help you in prayer this week?

ISSUES

MORAL ANGER

Introduction

"Row, row, row your boat ... Gently down the stream ... Merrily, merrily, merrily, merrily ... Life is but a dream." Well, maybe. Maybe not. Sometimes the current in the stream is going in the wrong direction, and you have to make a choice. In this Bible study, you will look at one of those times in the life of Jesus when he had to make a choice ... and upset a few people.

In biblical times, the people were required to sacrifice animals in the temple. If you were very poor, your sacrifice could be a dove which you could buy at the temple. Merchants had turned this into a profit-making business, and because local currency had to be used, travelers were forced to deal with money changers who ripped them off in the exchange. In addition, these chaotic activities took place in the court of the Gentiles, the only part of the temple in which God-fearing non-Jews could worship and pray.

Now, listen to the Bible story. Then, quickly move into groups of 4 and discuss the questionnaire.

JESUS CLEARS THE TEMPLE

¹⁵On reaching Jerusalem, Jesus entered the temple area and began driving out those who were buying and selling there. He overturned the tables of the money changers and the benches of those selling doves, ¹⁶and would not allow anyone to carry merchandise through the temple courts. ¹⁷And as he taught them, he said, "Is it not written:

> *" 'My house will be called*
> *a house of prayer for all nations'?*

But you have made it 'a den of robbers.' "

¹⁸The chief priests and the teachers of the law heard this and began looking for a way to kill him, for they feared him, because the whole crowd was amazed at his teaching.

Mark 11:15–18

1. Who does Jesus remind you of in this story?
- ❑ a bouncer
- ❑ a fiery prophet
- ❑ a Marine sergeant
- ❑ a political activist
- ❑ a bull in a china shop

2. How surprising is it to you to see Jesus turning over tables and driving money changers out of the temple?
   - ❏ very much
   - ❏ a little bit
   - ❏ none at all

3. When you see something wrong, are you more likely to act without thinking or think without acting?

4. If Jesus came to clean up your town, where would he start?
   - ❏ porno shops
   - ❏ newspaper / TV station
   - ❏ drug houses and corners
   - ❏ city hall
   - ❏ my school or workplace
   - ❏ my church
   - ❏ my home

5. In your school or work, what makes you angry because it is clearly wrong, unethical or immoral?

6. If Jesus came to your school or workplace, what would he do?
   - ❏ congratulate the people in charge on their moral values
   - ❏ overturn a few tables
   - ❏ hang out with the "sinners"
   - ❏ start a Bible study
   - ❏ become class president or CEO—where he could have influence
   - ❏ befriend the lonely and discouraged
   - ❏ stay quiet and set a good example
   - ❏ He wouldn't come to my school or workplace.

7. In each of the following categories, choose between the two options.

   I AM MORE LIKELY TO GET INVOLVED IN ISSUES THAT ...

   threaten my own life_____threaten the life or
   or interests   interests of others

   involve physical health _____involve moral health
   or well-being   or well-being

   my friends are _____my family is
   concerned about   concerned about

8. Which of these issues would you get involved in? Choose the top three.

___ world hunger

___ peace and justice issues

___ banning smoking in public places

___ passing out condoms in schools

___ fighting pornography

___ promoting prayer and Bible reading in school

___ freedom not to wear motorcycle helmets

___ legalizing marijuana for medical uses

___ income tax break for private school tuition

___ fighting discrimination and racism

___ abortion

___ environmental issues

___ keeping child molesters in jail

9. How would you describe yourself on taking a stand that could lead to conflict? Choose a number from 1 to 10 below.

PEACE AT ANY PRICE 1   2   3   4   5   6   7   8   9   10 LET'S HAVE IT OUT

10. How much does your spiritual commitment influence the way you stand on moral issues?

❏ a lot

❏ some

❏ not much

❏ I've never thought about it.

11. Where do you need to take a righteous stand? What is keeping you from doing so? How can this group support you in prayer?

ISSUES

RACISM AND PREJUDICE

Introduction

Have you ever felt shut out ... not invited to the party because of ... ? Well, this is what this study is all about. The Bible story is about a revelation made to the apostle Peter when the church was still young. In the orthodox Judaism of the time, food was considered "unclean" (religiously unacceptable) if it was from certain animals. In the same way, certain people were religiously unacceptable to them—in particular Gentiles, people who were foreigners and not raised in their religious traditions. Peter found that in Christ this was going to change.

Just prior to this passage, God had given a God-fearing Gentile by the name of Cornelius a vision. In the vision, an angel of God told this Roman army officer to send for Peter. Listen to the Bible story. Then, move into groups of 4 and discuss the questionnaire.

PETER'S VISION

⁹About noon the following day as they were on their journey and approaching the city, Peter went up on the roof to pray. ¹⁰He became hungry and wanted something to eat, and while the meal was being prepared, he fell into a trance. ¹¹He saw heaven opened and something like a large sheet being let down to earth by its four corners. ¹²It contained all kinds of four-footed animals, as well as reptiles of the earth and birds of the air. ¹³Then a voice told him, "Get up, Peter. Kill and eat."

¹⁴"Surely not, Lord!" Peter replied. "I have never eaten anything impure or unclean."

¹⁵The voice spoke to him a second time, "Do not call anything impure that God has made clean."

¹⁶This happened three times, and immediately the sheet was taken back to heaven.

¹⁷While Peter was wondering about the meaning of the vision, the men sent by Cornelius found out where Simon's house was and stopped at the gate. ¹⁸They called out, asking if Simon who was known as Peter was staying there.

¹⁹While Peter was still thinking about the vision, the Spirit said to him, "Simon, three men are looking for you. ²⁰So get up and go downstairs. Do not hesitate to go with them, for I have sent them." ...

²⁵As Peter entered the house, Cornelius met him and fell at his feet in reverence. ²⁶But Peter made him get up. "Stand up," he said, "I am only a man myself."

²⁷Talking with him, Peter went inside and found a large gathering of people. ²⁸He said to them: "You are well aware that it is against our law for a Jew to associate with a Gentile or visit him. But God has shown me that I should not call any man impure or unclean. ²⁹So when I was sent for, I came without raising any objection. May I ask why you sent for me?"

Acts 10:9–20,25–29

1. What immediately strikes you in this Bible story?
   - ❏ the attitude of Peter toward Gentiles
   - ❏ the spiritual desire of Cornelius the Gentile
   - ❏ the way God communicated through visions
   - ❏ the willingness of Peter to break the rules

2. If a sheet were to drop from heaven with all the foods on your "avoid" list, what would be on the sheet?
   - ❏ meat
   - ❏ vegetables
   - ❏ high-fat foods
   - ❏ health foods
   - ❏ anything not sold at McDonald's
   - ❏ anchovy pizza
   - ❏ sushi
   - ❏ raw oysters
   - ❏ other:_____

3. Imagine you are Peter. First you are told in a vision to eat meat that Jews are forbidden to eat. Now God tells you to go visit a Gentile, who was also considered impure or unclean. How are you feeling?
   - ❏ cautious
   - ❏ excited
   - ❏ confused
   - ❏ angry
   - ❏ fearful
   - ❏ awkward

4. What kind of person would you have the most trouble going to if God asked you to go to his or her house and give help?
   - ❏ a person of another race
   - ❏ a homosexual
   - ❏ a person who lives in a dirty, smelly house
   - ❏ a person who lives in a wealthy, exclusive neighborhood
   - ❏ an atheist
   - ❏ a person with AIDS
   - ❏ a person who speaks another language
   - ❏ other:_____

5. Being totally honest, what kind of walls have you permitted between yourself and others?
   - ❏ racial
   - ❏ moral
   - ❏ religious
   - ❏ political
   - ❏ economic
   - ❏ denominational
   - ❏ other:_____

6. What's the most common reason you feel excluded from a group?
   - ☐ race
   - ☐ religion
   - ☐ social status
   - ☐ interests / abilities
   - ☐ cliques
   - ☐ career
   - ☐ other:_____

7. If you were put in charge of reconciliation in your school or community, what would you do?

8. What people wouldn't feel at home in your group or church?
   - ☐ people from the other side of the tracks
   - ☐ people of a different color or ethnic background
   - ☐ people who don't wear our kind of clothes
   - ☐ people who are not very religious
   - ☐ people who are too religious
   - ☐ people who are down-and-out
   - ☐ people who are upper class
   - ☐ other:_____

9. What can your group or church do to help those people feel accepted?

10. If God gave you personally a vision about your attitude toward other people, what would he tell you?

11. Respond to that message in prayer. How else would you like the group to pray for you?

ISSUES

VIOLENCE AND APATHY

Introduction

Violence and apathy are not new. In the time of Jesus in the first century, there was a road that was so notorious for assault and murder that Jesus used it in the parable about the Good Samaritan. (Samaritans were people the Jews despised as half-breeds both physically and spiritually.) Roving gangs would ambush pedestrians on their way to or from Jericho. Often one of the gang would lay down on the side of the road as though they were injured. Then, when a pedestrian stopped to help, the rest of the gang would jump out of the shadows and assault the would-be helper.

Jewish priests and Levites (assistants to the priests) would have been concerned about getting too close to a dead mugging victim. According to the Law of Moses, touching a corpse would have made them "unclean" and unable to perform their religious duties. As you listen to this parable, try to imagine what you would do in this situation. Then, move into groups of 4 and discuss the questionnaire.

THE PARABLE OF THE GOOD SAMARITAN

25On one occasion an expert in the law stood up to test Jesus. "Teacher," he asked, "what must I do to inherit eternal life?"

26"What is written in the Law?" he replied. "How do you read it?"

27He answered: " 'Love the Lord your God with all your heart and with all your soul and with all your strength and with all your mind'; and 'Love your neighbor as yourself.' "

28"You have answered correctly," Jesus replied. "Do this and you will live."

29But he wanted to justify himself, so he asked Jesus, "And who is my neighbor?"

30In reply Jesus said: "A man was going down from Jerusalem to Jericho, when he fell into the hands of robbers. They stripped him of his clothes, beat him and went away, leaving him half dead. 31A priest happened to be going down the same road, and when he saw the man, he passed by on the other side. 32So too, a Levite, when he came to the place and saw him, passed by on the other side. 33But a Samaritan, as he traveled, came where the man was; and when he saw him, he took pity on him. 34He went to him and bandaged his wounds, pouring on oil and wine. Then he put the man on his own donkey, took him to an inn and took care of him. 35The next day he took out two silver coins and gave them to the innkeeper. 'Look after him,' he said, 'and when I return, I will reimburse you for any extra expense you may have.'

36"Which of these three do you think was a neighbor to the man who fell into the hands of robbers?"

37The expert in the law replied, "The one who had mercy on him."
Jesus told him, "Go and do likewise."

Luke 10:25–37

1. How would the media respond if something like the story in this parable happened today?
   ❑ The violence would make big news.
   ❑ The apathy would make big news.
   ❑ It would be ignored because stuff like this is so common.

2. Have you ever helped a stranger or been helped by a stranger? What happened?

3. If you were on your way to an important appointment and saw someone who looked beat up (but you didn't know if they were faking it or not), what would you do?
   ❑ find someone to check it out
   ❑ pass on by
   ❑ stop and try to help
   ❑ call 911

4. After reading this parable, who would you say is your "neighbor"?
   ❑ any person in need
   ❑ those I have a reasonable hope of being able to help
   ❑ those I'm most afraid of helping
   ❑ everyone—even my enemies

5. If Jesus wanted to bring home to your community the same lesson as he did in this story, what place would he use?
   ❑ one of our dangerous inner city streets
   ❑ a convenience store
   ❑ a public park
   ❑ the street in front of the high school
   ❑ the parking lot at the mall
   ❑ We don't have any place like that in our town.
   ❑ Any street will do; they are all unsafe.

6. What is the scariest form of violence in your city?
   ❑ drive-by shootings
   ❑ sex clubs / gang rape
   ❑ child abuse
   ❑ vandalism / burning of church property
   ❑ drug or turf wars
   ❑ date rape
   ❑ other:_____

7. What are you doing about the situation?
   - ❒ I just try to stay out of the way.
   - ❒ I support the police department.
   - ❒ I pray God will keep my family safe.
   - ❒ I don't go through certain neighborhoods at night.
   - ❒ I try to stand up and be counted.

8. If the Good Samaritan came to your city, what would he do about these problems?
   - ❒ He would pass by on the other side.
   - ❒ He would get involved in criminal rehabilitation programs.
   - ❒ He would get our church to do something for broken families.
   - ❒ He would get our schools to offer help for young kids before they turn to violence.
   - ❒ He would hire a crisis counselor.
   - ❒ other:_____

9. On a scale of 1 (low) to 10 (high), rate yourself on the first part of verse 27: "Love the Lord your God with all your heart and with all your soul and with all your strength and with all your mind."

10. Using the same scale, rate yourself on the second part of verse 27: "Love your neighbor as yourself."

11. How can this group help you in prayer this week?

SEXUAL DESIRES

Introduction

Many people consider David their favorite character in the Bible. He was a musician, a poet, a military genius and the greatest leader the nation of Israel ever produced. As a teenager, he volunteered to fight Goliath for the honor of God and his country, and he defeated the giant.

But he had one weakness, and he let it get the best of him. We are going to pick up the story of David and Bathsheba at the time of the year when the king usually went with his army to battle, but David stayed home and let his general lead the army. Listen to the story and move into groups of 4 to discuss the questionnaire.

DAVID AND BATHSHEBA

11 *In the spring, at the time when kings go off to war, David sent Joab out with the king's men and the whole Israelite army. They destroyed the Ammonites and besieged Rabbah. But David remained in Jerusalem.*

²One evening David got up from his bed and walked around on the roof of the palace. From the roof he saw a woman bathing. The woman was very beautiful, ³and David sent someone to find out about her. The man said, "Isn't this Bathsheba, the daughter of Eliam and the wife of Uriah the Hittite?" ⁴Then David sent messengers to get her. She came to him, and he slept with her. (She had purified herself from her uncleanness.) Then she went back home. ⁵The woman conceived and sent word to David, saying, "I am pregnant."

⁶So David sent this word to Joab: "Send me Uriah the Hittite." And Joab sent him to David. ⁷When Uriah came to him, David asked him how Joab was, how the soldiers were and how the war was going. ⁸Then David said to Uriah, "Go down to your house and wash your feet." So Uriah left the palace, and a gift from the king was sent after him. ⁹But Uriah slept at the entrance to the palace with all his master's servants and did not go down to his house.

¹⁰When David was told, "Uriah did not go home," he asked him, "Haven't you just come from a distance? Why didn't you go home?"

¹¹Uriah said to David, "The ark and Israel and Judah are staying in tents, and my master Joab and my lord's men are camped in the open fields. How could I go to my house to eat and drink and lie with my wife? As surely as you live, I will not do such a thing!"

¹²Then David said to him, "Stay here one more day, and tomorrow I will send you back." So Uriah remained in Jerusalem that day and the next. ¹³At David's invitation, he ate and drank with him, and David made him drunk. But in the evening Uriah went out to sleep on his mat among his master's servants; he did not go home.

¹⁴In the morning David wrote a letter to Joab and sent it with Uriah. ¹⁵In it he wrote, "Put Uriah in the front line where the fighting is fiercest. Then withdraw from him so he will be struck down and die."

16So while Joab had the city under siege, he put Uriah at a place where he knew the strongest defenders were. 17When the men of the city came out and fought against Joab, some of the men in David's army fell; moreover, Uriah the Hittite died.

2 Samuel 11:1–17

1. This story happened in the spring. Who was your first "crush" or what was your worst case of "spring fever"?

2. Imagine that this scandal had occurred today between a woman and a major political figure. Which of the following scenarios would you expect?
   ❒ Everyone would say, "Ho, hum—again?"
   ❒ Their pictures would be splashed on all the papers.
   ❒ The politician would categorically deny it.
   ❒ The woman would be cast as a bimbo and the villainess.
   ❒ They would both write about it and have competing best-sellers.
   ❒ It would be one of those scandals that quickly fades from the news.

3. Since God created David with sexual urges, when did his thoughts or actions become sin?
   ❒ when he didn't go with the army like he should have
   ❒ when he saw Bathsheba taking a bath
   ❒ when he sent someone to find out about her
   ❒ when he sent messengers to get her
   ❒ when he made love to her

4. How do you imagine Bathsheba felt about this whole affair?
   ❒ used
   ❒ swept off her feet
   ❒ flattered
   ❒ forced against her will
   ❒ guilty

5. How do you feel about God's standards for sexual purity? Choose one of the two options in each of the following pairs. God's standards are:

   clear_____unclear
   outdated _____relevant
   attainable _____unattainable
   for our good _____unnecessary

6. How can a relationship with God influence the way we handle our sexual desires? What advice would you give a friend who is caught up with pornography or sexual immorality?

7. When do you find yourself most vulnerable to temptation?
- ❏ when I'm bored
- ❏ when I'm under a lot of stress
- ❏ when I let my mind dwell on certain things
- ❏ when I'm away from home
- ❏ after a spiritual high
- ❏ other:_____

8. Where do you need to set some boundaries for what you are going to watch, read and see?

9. On a scale of 1 (great) to 10 (terrible), how would you rate your spiritual life right now? How can the group pray for you?

10. How can this group remember you in prayer this week?

ISSUES

CULTS / OCCULT

Introduction

Welcome to the crazy world called modern religion. We've got horoscopes and tarot cards, Ouija boards and crystals, satanic music and horror movies, witchcraft and seances, and a library of science fiction books and videos that introduce you to the dark side of the spiritual world. And we have groups like the Branch Davidians, Moonies, the Children of God and Heaven's Gate who promise you spiritual ecstasy and live-in family if you will only turn over your mind and all of your possessions to them. What a deal!

In this Bible study, you will take on the issue of cults, the occult, counterfeits and New Age religions. The Bible story is familiar. It is the story of the temptation of Jesus by Satan right after he was baptized. In the three temptations, you will discover a lot of the temptations that the cults and counterfeits offer to every seeker after spiritual truth. Listen to the story. Then, move into groups of 4 and discuss the following questionnaire and case studies.

THE TEMPTATION OF JESUS

4 Then Jesus was led by the Spirit into the desert to be tempted by the devil. ²After fasting forty days and forty nights, he was hungry. ³The tempter came to him and said, "If you are the Son of God, tell these stones to become bread."

⁴Jesus answered, "It is written: 'Man does not live on bread alone, but on every word that comes from the mouth of God.' "

⁵Then the devil took him to the holy city and had him stand on the highest point of the temple. ⁶"If you are the Son of God," he said, "throw yourself down. For it is written:

" 'He will command his angels concerning you,
  and they will lift you up in their hands,
 so that you will not strike your foot against a stone.' "

⁷Jesus answered him, "It is also written: 'Do not put the Lord your God to the test.' "

⁸Again, the devil took him to a very high mountain and showed him all the kingdoms of the world and their splendor. ⁹"All this I will give you," he said, "if you will bow down and worship me."

¹⁰Jesus said to him, "Away from me, Satan! For it is written: 'Worship the Lord your God, and serve him only.' "

¹¹Then the devil left him, and angels came and attended him.

Matthew 4:1–11

1. Who does the devil remind you of in this story?
   - ❐ a prostitute
   - ❐ a drug pusher
   - ❐ a corrupt politician
   - ❐ a pushy used-car salesman
   - ❐ the emperor in *Star Wars*
   - ❐ someone much more subtle

2. How vulnerable to temptation was Jesus?
   - ❐ He was just as vulnerable as I am.
   - ❐ He was vulnerable, but in a different way.
   - ❐ He really wasn't vulnerable at all.

3. What do you do when you are approached by someone from a cult?

CASE STUDIES

Case Study #1: Jeff

Jeff was an outgoing, fun-loving, handsome guy. At school he was into everything. He had lots of friends, was a good student and was fun to be around. But something went wrong. One spring he became interested in magic and some of the mystical things mentioned in his science fiction books. His parents had divorced and he wanted to escape from the pain. When his mother objected to some of the books on horoscopes and the occult he was reading, he got angry and threatened to move out. He retreated to his headphones and his music.

Things are not much better now. His sparkle and charm are gone. He has shut off most of his old friends and withdrawn more into himself. His friends are boring, he thinks school is a drag ... and he seems to spend a lot of time reading about mediums and people who can contact the spirit world. He is fascinated with occult symbols like the scarab, the skull and the Southern Cross.

Case Study #2: Simone

Simone also was an outgoing, fun person to be around. She did certain things well, but school was a struggle for her. So, her mom enrolled her in an after-school program off-campus that was supposed to improve her learning skills and self-esteem toward higher academic achievement. During the sessions, however, she was led into heavy meditation, visualization (meant to alter the way one thinks), and was told she could have a spirit-guide to go with her on the mental journeys. She was told she had unlimited potential if she would just tap into the power within her.

Her grades didn't improve, and she got into heavy drug use as well as promiscuous, even abusive, relationships. By age 18 she signed her name in blood to join a witches coven that practiced white magic (magic for "positive" purposes). While this was not the type of coven involved in animal sacrifices and destructive acts, they did come in contact with the darker types of occult groups. Who knows where Simone would have ended up had she not come in contact with a group of Christians who shared God's truth and love with her.

4. Have you ever run across someone like Jeff or Simone? How did they make you feel? How did they get in the occult?

5. How did you deal with the situation? How can Jesus Christ meet the needs of someone attracted to the occult?

6. Have you had any contact or personal experience with any of the following, and, if so, what was the experience like?

___ tarot cards	___ satanic / horror flicks
___ Ouija boards	___ horoscopes
___ seances	___ mind control
___ Yoga / Eastern meditation	___ spirit-guides
___ satanic music	___ astrology
___ witchcraft	___ crystals
___ occultic literature	___ New Age philosophies
___ Dungeon and Dragons, etc.	___ cults / false religions

7. If the devil had three "shots" at you, which area of your life would he focus on?
   - ❑ spiritual temptations
   - ❑ physical temptations
   - ❑ financial temptations
   - ❑ ambition / power
   - ❑ my self-identity
   - ❑ other:_____

8. How do you deal with temptation?
   - ❑ give in to it
   - ❑ fight it off
   - ❑ beat myself up with guilt
   - ❑ just say "no"
   - ❑ do something to get my mind off of it
   - ❑ ask for God's help
   - ❑ talk to someone about it
   - ❑ other:_____

9. What has helped you overcome temptation when it comes?
   - ❑ Scripture
   - ❑ telling someone about it
   - ❑ talking myself out of it
   - ❑ prayer
   - ❑ running away
   - ❑ other:_____

10. How can this group pray for you—specifically in the area of temptation?

MY SPIRITUAL JOURNEY

Introduction

To answer some of his critics who thought he was running around with the wrong people, Jesus told a story about a wayward son and a father who threw a party for this son when he came home.

As you listen to this familiar story again, try to put yourself in the situation of all three characters: the father, the younger brother, and the older brother. Then, move into groups of 4 and discuss the questionnaire.

THE PARABLE OF THE LOST SON

[11]*Jesus continued: "There was a man who had two sons.* [12]*The younger one said to his father, 'Father, give me my share of the estate.' So he divided his property between them.*

[13]*"Not long after that, the younger son got together all he had, set off for a distant country and there squandered his wealth in wild living.* [14]*After he had spent everything, there was a severe famine in that whole country, and he began to be in need.* [15]*So he went and hired himself out to a citizen of that country, who sent him to his fields to feed pigs.* [16]*He longed to fill his stomach with the pods that the pigs were eating, but no one gave him anything.*

[17]*"When he came to his senses, he said, 'How many of my father's hired men have food to spare, and here I am starving to death!* [18]*I will set out and go back to my father and say to him: Father, I have sinned against heaven and against you.* [19]*I am no longer worthy to be called your son; make me like one of your hired men.'* [20]*So he got up and went to his father.*

"But while he was still a long way off, his father saw him and was filled with compassion for him; he ran to his son, threw his arms around him and kissed him.

[21]*"The son said to him, 'Father, I have sinned against heaven and against you. I am no longer worthy to be called your son.'*

[22]*"But the father said to his servants, 'Quick! Bring the best robe and put it on him. Put a ring on his finger and sandals on his feet.* [23]*Bring the fattened calf and kill it. Let's have a feast and celebrate.* [24]*For this son of mine was dead and is alive again; he was lost and is found.' So they began to celebrate.*

[25]*"Meanwhile, the older son was in the field. When he came near the house, he heard music and dancing.* [26]*So he called one of the servants and asked him what was going on.* [27]*'Your brother has come,' he replied, 'and your father has killed the fattened calf because he has him back safe and sound.'*

[28]*"The older brother became angry and refused to go in. So his father went out and pleaded with him.* [29]*But he answered his father, 'Look! All these years I've been slaving for you and never disobeyed your orders. Yet you never gave me even a young goat so I could celebrate with my friends.* [30]*But when this son of yours who*

has squandered your property with prostitutes comes home, you kill the fattened calf for him!

[31]" 'My son,' the father said, 'you are always with me, and everything I have is yours. [32]But we had to celebrate and be glad, because this brother of yours was dead and is alive again; he was lost and is found.' "

Luke 15:11–32

1. Where are you in the birth order of your family?
   - ❏ oldest
   - ❏ youngest
   - ❏ in the middle
   - ❏ I'm an only child.

2. When was the first time you thought about leaving home? Did you do it?

3. If you had been the father in this Bible story, what would you have said to the younger son when he asked for his inheritance early in order to leave home?
   - ❏ "Are you crazy?!"
   - ❏ "Why you ungrateful ... !!"
   - ❏ "Well, I'm disappointed, but here you are."
   - ❏ "No problem, son."

4. If you had been the father and had a pretty good idea where your son had gone, would you have gone after him?
   - ❏ Yes, you don't want to see your kid get in trouble.
   - ❏ Maybe, if I thought I could get him to come home.
   - ❏ No, you have to let people make their own mistakes.
   - ❏ It all depends.

5. What is the closest you have come to going through a wild period like the young man in this story?

6. Of the two sons, which reminds you the most of your own spiritual story?
   - ❏ the son who left home at an early age—and came back
   - ❏ the son who did not leave home—but felt left out of his father's party

7. When did you spiritually "leave home" in your relationship with God, and what caused the comeback?

8. If you could compare your spiritual journey to this story, where are you right now?
   - ❐ just leaving home
   - ❐ in a far country
   - ❐ on my way back home

9. How do you sense God calling you to get closer to him? What will you do to respond?

10. How do you feel about sharing your spiritual journey like this with your group? How can the group pray for you?

SPIRITUAL FORMATION

FORGIVENESS OF SINS

Introduction

This Bible study is about the crucifixion of Jesus Christ, because you can't talk about the forgiveness of sins without giving the explanation—that somebody had to pay the price. And that somebody had to be sinless. And that person was Jesus—"the Lamb of God." Right now, you are going to look at the death of Jesus as a historical record.

Listen to the story of the crucifixion and death of Christ. Then, move into groups of 4 and discuss the questionnaire.

THE CRUCIFIXION AND DEATH OF JESUS

32Two other men, both criminals, were also led out with him to be executed. 33When they came to the place called the Skull, there they crucified him, along with the criminals—one on his right, the other on his left. 34Jesus said, "Father, forgive them, for they do not know what they are doing." And they divided up his clothes by casting lots.

35The people stood watching, and the rulers even sneered at him. They said, "He saved others; let him save himself if he is the Christ of God, the Chosen One."

36The soldiers also came up and mocked him. They offered him wine vinegar 37and said, "If you are the king of the Jews, save yourself."

38There was a written notice above him, which read: THIS IS THE KING OF THE JEWS.

39One of the criminals who hung there hurled insults at him: "Aren't you the Christ? Save yourself and us!"

40But the other criminal rebuked him. "Don't you fear God," he said, "since you are under the same sentence? 41We are punished justly, for we are getting what our deeds deserve. But this man has done nothing wrong."

42Then he said, "Jesus, remember me when you come into your kingdom."

43Jesus answered him, "I tell you the truth, today you will be with me in paradise."

44It was now about the sixth hour, and darkness came over the whole land until the ninth hour, 45for the sun stopped shining. And the curtain of the temple was torn in two. 46Jesus called out with a loud voice, "Father, into your hands I commit my spirit." When he had said this, he breathed his last.

47The centurion, seeing what had happened, praised God and said, "Surely this was a righteous man." 48When all the people who had gathered to witness this sight saw what took place, they beat their breasts and went away. 49But all those who knew him, including the women who had followed him from Galilee, stood at a distance, watching these things.

Luke 23:32–49

1. If you were the editor of the *Jerusalem Times*, what headline would you pick to describe the events of the death of Christ?
   ❑ "Daytime Darkness Descends"
   ❑ "Crucifixion Stuns City"
   ❑ "Self-Proclaimed Messiah Killed"
   ❑ "Temple Curtain Ruined"

2. If the following people were interviewed for your newspaper coverage of Jesus' crucifixion, whose opinion would you personally share?
   ❑ the followers of Jesus—despairing of all hope
   ❑ those who made fun of Jesus—unable to see the purpose of Jesus' suffering and death
   ❑ the centurion—understanding suddenly who Jesus really was

3. What would be most likely to make *you* proclaim publicly (like the centurion), in the presence of your friends, "Surely this was a righteous man"?
   ❑ a lot of scary signs, like those that happened that day
   ❑ feeling forgiven for all the bad things I've done
   ❑ seeing how badly my friends need Christ
   ❑ No way I'd *ever* say such a thing!
   ❑ I say it all the time already.

4. In the midst of such pain and ridicule, how could Jesus say, "Father, forgive them"? How do these words make you feel?

5. How easy is it for you to forgive people who hurt you?

6. When did you come to realize that Jesus died for you and for the forgiveness of your sins?

7. How does it make you feel when you think about what God has done for you through the death of Jesus Christ on the cross?
   ❑ guilty   ❑ grateful
   ❑ interested   ❑ uncomfortable
   ❑ relieved   ❑ loved
   ❑ I've heard all of this before.   ❑ doubtful

8. How would you describe the difference that Christ's death and God's forgiveness has made in the way you live your life?
   - ❑ a little bit
   - ❑ a whole lot
   - ❑ not as much as it should
   - ❑ a lot more than it used to
   - ❑ I'm not sure.

9. Are you closer to Christ now than you were five years ago? If yes, in what way? If no, explain why.

10. If you could invite one person to join your group—someone who really needs Christ—who would you like to invite?

11. How can this group remember you in prayer this week?

SPIRITUAL FORMATION

TURNING AROUND

Introduction

This Bible story is a familiar one—the conversion of the apostle Paul. Paul (whose name was Saul until he became a Christian) grew up as a very religious person. In fact, in his early life, he led the persecution of Christians and was involved in the stoning of a Christian by the name of Stephen. But God brought this guy to the ground and turned him around.

Listen to the story. Then, move into groups of 4 and discuss the questionnaire.

SAUL'S CONVERSION

9 Meanwhile, Saul was still breathing out murderous threats against the Lord's disciples. He went to the high priest ²and asked him for letters to the synagogues in Damascus, so that if he found any there who belonged to the Way, whether men or women, he might take them as prisoners to Jerusalem. ³As he neared Damascus on his journey, suddenly a light from heaven flashed around him. ⁴He fell to the ground and heard a voice say to him, "Saul, Saul, why do you persecute me?"

⁵"Who are you, Lord?" Saul asked.

"I am Jesus, whom you are persecuting," he replied. ⁶"Now get up and go into the city, and you will be told what you must do."

⁷The men traveling with Saul stood there speechless; they heard the sound but did not see anyone. ⁸Saul got up from the ground, but when he opened his eyes he could see nothing. So they led him by the hand into Damascus. ⁹For three days he was blind, and did not eat or drink anything.

¹⁰In Damascus there was a disciple named Ananias. The Lord called to him in a vision, "Ananias!"

"Yes, Lord," he answered.

¹¹The Lord told him, "Go to the house of Judas on Straight Street and ask for a man from Tarsus named Saul, for he is praying. ¹²In a vision he has seen a man named Ananias come and place his hands on him to restore his sight." ...

¹⁷Then Ananias went to the house and entered it. Placing his hands on Saul, he said, "Brother Saul, the Lord—Jesus, who appeared to you on the road as you were coming here—has sent me so that you may see again and be filled with the Holy Spirit." ¹⁸Immediately, something like scales fell from Saul's eyes, and he could see again. He got up and was baptized, ¹⁹and after taking some food, he regained his strength.

Acts 9:1–12,17–19

1. How would the medical profession today explain what happened to Saul (Paul) on the road to Damascus?
   - ❐ He was struck by lightning.
   - ❐ He had a physical breakdown.
   - ❐ He had a mental breakdown.
   - ❐ He had a partial stroke that rendered him temporarily blind.
   - ❐ He had a psychological crisis due to an overly-religious personality.
   - ❐ He suffered from repressed guilt for his role in persecuting people.

2. How would you feel if you were Paul during the three days that he sat in his room in Damascus—blind—trying to figure out what had happened to him?
   - ❐ wiped out
   - ❐ confused
   - ❐ terrified
   - ❐ humbled
   - ❐ angry
   - ❐ repentant

3. If you could compare your spiritual journey to Paul's experience, where are you right now?
   - ❐ on the road to Damascus
   - ❐ starting to hear God call out my name and wondering what God is trying to tell me
   - ❐ experiencing some of the same emotions Paul went through
   - ❐ trying to sort out what has been happening

4. How would you compare your conversion to Paul's conversion?
   - ❐ Mine was more gradual.
   - ❐ Mine was more intellectual.
   - ❐ Mine was different, but just as real.
   - ❐ Mine was even more dramatic.
   - ❐ I'm on my way back to God and I still have a lot of questions.

5. Ananias was sent by God to come alongside of Paul in his crisis. Who has come alongside of you to help you sort out what is going on?
   - ❐ my parent(s) / spouse
   - ❐ a teacher
   - ❐ my brother / sister
   - ❐ one or two friends
   - ❐ another relative
   - ❐ no one
   - ❐ my group leader / pastor
   - ❐ other:_____

6. If you had to explain to little children how God turned your life around, how would you describe it?
   ❏ It is like getting to know a friend.
   ❏ It is like waking up one morning and being a different person.
   ❏ It is like coming into the world as a baby.
   ❏ It is like a bolt of lightning.
   ❏ It is like getting a puppy for your birthday.
   ❏ It is like:_____

7. How were others able to notice the difference in your life after you met Jesus?

8. In what area of your life have you seen the most change since you committed your life to Christ?
   ❏ my beliefs   ❏ my priorities
   ❏ my relationships   ❏ my attitudes
   ❏ my goals   ❏ my values
   ❏ my habits / lifestyle   ❏ other:_____
   ❏ my devotional life (prayer, Bible study)

9. What changes do you feel God is calling you to make in your life now?

10. How would you like the group to pray for you this week?

SPIRITUAL FORMATION

DEALING WITH DOUBT

Introduction

Sooner or later, every Christian will have spiritual struggles and doubts—when you feel like your prayers go no higher than the ceiling. Someone you love dies unexpectedly and you wonder if God is asleep on the job. You are disappointed in a relationship—and you wonder if God cares.

This is what this Bible study is all about—spiritual struggles and doubts. The story in the Bible that you will look at is the story of Thomas—often called "Doubting Thomas." For some reason, he was not in the room after the Resurrection when Jesus appeared to the disciples. And he refused to believe them when they said Jesus was alive. Listen to the story. Then, move into groups of 4 and discuss the questionnaire.

JESUS APPEARS TO THOMAS

24Now Thomas (called Didymus), one of the Twelve, was not with the disciples when Jesus came. 25So the other disciples told him, "We have seen the Lord!"
But he said to them, "Unless I see the nail marks in his hands and put my finger where the nails were, and put my hand into his side, I will not believe it."

26A week later his disciples were in the house again, and Thomas was with them. Though the doors were locked, Jesus came and stood among them and said, "Peace be with you!" 27Then he said to Thomas, "Put your finger here; see my hands. Reach out your hand and put it into my side. Stop doubting and believe."

28Thomas said to him, "My Lord and my God!"

29Then Jesus told him, "Because you have seen me, you have believed; blessed are those who have not seen and yet have believed."

John 20:24–29

1. Who or what would you believe most?
   ❏ news reporter
   ❏ sales advertisements
   ❏ police radar
   ❏ psychic hotline

2. What would convince you to believe that someone really came back from the dead?
   ❏ a death certificate
   ❏ eyewitnesses
   ❏ firsthand knowledge of the person before and after
   ❏ pictures in the *National Enquirer*

3. "Unless I see the nail marks in his hands and put my finger where the nails were, and put my hand into his side, I will not believe it." What was Thomas saying?
   - ❏ "You guys are crazy."
   - ❏ "I need proof."
   - ❏ "I want to believe, but ..."
   - ❏ "Don't break my heart again."

4. Who does Thomas remind you of in this story?
   - ❏ a science teacher
   - ❏ an agnostic
   - ❏ an honest person who wanted to believe
   - ❏ a friend of mine
   - ❏ myself
   - ❏ other:_____

5. What is the closest that you have come to going through what Thomas went through?
   - ❏ when my parents or I went through a divorce
   - ❏ when someone close to me died
   - ❏ when I dropped out of Christian fellowship
   - ❏ when I tried really hard but failed
   - ❏ when I was disappointed and took it out on God
   - ❏ other:_____

6. How do you think Jesus feels when we have doubts about our faith?
   - ❏ angry—"I can't believe you have doubts!"
   - ❏ disappointed—"How could you question me?"
   - ❏ ready—"Bring it on, I can handle your questions!"
   - ❏ glad—"I'm happy you are curious about me."
   - ❏ other:_____

7. What do you rely upon for spiritual "proof"?
   - ❏ gut feelings
   - ❏ what the Bible says
   - ❏ what my church teaches
   - ❏ logic and common sense
   - ❏ emotional peace
   - ❏ Christian family and friends
   - ❏ simple faith
   - ❏ other:_____

8. When you have struggles and doubts in your faith, what have you found most helpful?

❐ going to the Bible

❐ talking it over with my pastor

❐ sharing my struggles with my family and friends

❐ letting my family and friends share their struggles

❐ going to church / small group / youth group

❐ going ahead "on faith"

❐ spending time alone with God

❐ being encouraged by the faith of others

❐ other:_____

9. If you could ask Jesus one "hard question" about your spiritual life, what would it be?

❐ How do I deal with doubt?

❐ How do I deal with guilt?

❐ What's wrong when I don't always *feel* like a Christian?

❐ Where is God when I'm hurting?

❐ Why can't I seem to get closer to you?

❐ other:_____

10. How would you describe your spiritual life right now?

❐ full of doubt

❐ full of faith

❐ half and half

❐ increasing in doubt

❐ increasing in faith

11. How can the group support you in prayer this week?

SPIRITUAL FORMATION

HEAVY STUFF

Introduction

There comes a time in the life of every Christian when you have to decide who is going to sit on the throne of your life—you or God.

Interestingly, Jesus had to face this very decision. He faced it just before he was arrested and taken away to be crucified. He was in a garden—praying. He knew that Judas had gone to get the temple police to arrest him. Jesus still had time to run away and avoid all the pain. But he had to decide. Immediately. Jesus took his three closest friends (Peter, James and John) with him to this garden to pray.

Listen to the story. Then, move into groups of 4 and discuss the questionnaire.

GETHSEMANE

³⁶Then Jesus went with his disciples to a place called Gethsemane, and he said to them, "Sit here while I go over there and pray." ³⁷He took Peter and the two sons of Zebedee along with him, and he began to be sorrowful and troubled. ³⁸Then he said to them, "My soul is overwhelmed with sorrow to the point of death. Stay here and keep watch with me."

³⁹Going a little farther, he fell with his face to the ground and prayed, "My Father, if it is possible, may this cup be taken from me. Yet not as I will, but as you will."

⁴⁰Then he returned to his disciples and found them sleeping, "Could you men not keep watch with me for one hour?" he asked Peter. ⁴¹"Watch and pray so that you will not fall into temptation. The spirit is willing, but the body is weak."

⁴²He went away a second time and prayed, "My Father, if it is not possible for this cup to be taken away unless I drink it, may your will be done."

⁴³When he came back, he again found them sleeping, because their eyes were heavy. ⁴⁴So he left them and went away once more and prayed the third time, saying the same thing.

⁴⁵Then he returned to the disciples and said to them, "Are you still sleeping and resting? Look, the hour is near, and the Son of Man is betrayed into the hands of sinners. ⁴⁶Rise, let us go! Here comes my betrayer!"

Matthew 26:36–46

1. When have you fallen asleep at a very embarrassing moment?
   - ❐ in church
   - ❐ in class or at work
   - ❐ on a date
   - ❐ during a concert or recital
   - ❐ other:_____

2. What was the hardest part of this experience for Jesus?
- ❒ being let down by his friends
- ❒ submitting to God's will
- ❒ preparing for the cross

3. Where is the "Garden of Gethsemane" that you go to when you're faced with making a big decision?
- ❒ my bedroom
- ❒ my favorite place outdoors
- ❒ church
- ❒ the ballpark
- ❒ I don't really have a place.
- ❒ other:_____

4. In the last 12 months, what is the closest you have come to facing your own personal Gethsemane—where you needed to submit to God's will and not yours?

5. What is the biggest issue you are facing in your spiritual life right now?
- ❒ sorting out my values
- ❒ choosing the right friends
- ❒ making time for God every day
- ❒ cleaning up my life / breaking some old habits
- ❒ sharing my faith openly
- ❒ knowing what God wants me to do with my life
- ❒ other:_____

6. What is harder for you?
- ❒ knowing what God wants me to do
- ❒ doing what I know God wants me to do
- ❒ standing alone when my friends or family don't support me
- ❒ being consistent

7. What have you found helpful in determining the will of God for your life?
- ❒ studying the Bible
- ❒ praying
- ❒ asking the counsel of another Christian
- ❒ attending church
- ❒ other:_____

8. When it comes to doing the will of God, how would you finish this sentence? "I desire to do God's will ..."
   - ❐ all of the time
   - ❐ most of the time
   - ❐ some of the time
   - ❐ rarely

9. What decision are you going to face in the near future where you need to seek God's will?

10. How can the group pray for this situation and for other needs in your life?

BELIEFS

GOD THE FATHER

Introduction

This Bible study is designed to help you understand the first statement in the Apostles' Creed: *"I believe in God, the Father Almighty, maker of heaven and earth."*

Listen to the story of Adam and Eve. Then, move into groups of 4 and discuss the questionnaire.

ADAM AND EVE

⁴This is the account of the heavens and the earth when they were created. When the LORD God made the earth and the heavens—⁵and no shrub of the field had yet appeared on the earth and no plant of the field had yet sprung up, for the LORD God had not sent rain on the earth and there was no man to work the ground, ⁶but streams came up from the earth and watered the whole surface of the ground—⁷the LORD God formed the man from the dust of the ground and breathed into his nostrils the breath of life, and the man became a living being.

⁸Now the LORD God had planted a garden in the east, in Eden; and there he put the man he had formed. ⁹And the LORD God made all kinds of trees grow out of the ground—trees that were pleasing to the eye and good for food. In the middle of the garden were the tree of life and the tree of the knowledge of good and evil.

¹⁰A river watering the garden flowed from Eden; from there it was separated into four headwaters. ¹¹The name of the first is the Pishon; it winds through the entire land of Havilah, where there is gold. ¹²(The gold of that land is good; aromatic resin and onyx are also there.) ¹³The name of the second river is the Gihon; it winds through the entire land of Cush. ¹⁴The name of the third river is the Tigris; it runs along the east side of Asshur. And the fourth river is the Euphrates.

¹⁵The LORD God took the man and put him in the Garden of Eden to work it and take care of it. ¹⁶And the LORD God commanded the man, "You are free to eat from any tree in the garden; ¹⁷but you must not eat from the tree of the knowledge of good and evil, for when you eat of it you will surely die."

¹⁸The LORD God said, "It is not good for the man to be alone. I will make a helper suitable for him."

¹⁹Now the LORD God had formed out of the ground all the beasts of the field and all the birds of the air. He brought them to the man to see what he would name them; and whatever the man called each living creature, that was its name. ²⁰So the man gave names to all the livestock, the birds of the air and all the beasts of the field.

But for Adam no suitable helper was found. ²¹So the LORD God caused the man to fall into a deep sleep; and while he was sleeping, he took one of the man's ribs and closed up the place with flesh. ²²Then the LORD God made a woman from the rib he had taken out of the man, and he brought her to the man.

23The man said,

> *"This is now bone of my bones*
> *and flesh of my flesh;*
> *she shall be called 'woman,'*
> *for she was taken out of man."*

24For this reason a man will leave his father and mother and be united to his wife, and they will become one flesh.

25The man and his wife were both naked, and they felt no shame.

Genesis 2:4–25

1. If you could have a snapshot showing just one moment in this creation story, what would it be?
   - ❏ when Adam came to life
   - ❏ when Eve came to life
   - ❏ a wide-angle view of the unspoiled Garden of Eden
   - ❏ the tree of the knowledge of good and evil
   - ❏ Adam and Eve seeing each other for the first time

2. What part of creation convinces you the most of God's existence?
   - ❏ the stars in the heavens
   - ❏ the majestic mountains
   - ❏ a newborn baby
   - ❏ a tiny, delicate flower
   - ❏ a beautiful rainbow
   - ❏ a soaring eagle

3. What do you think most of the people around you (job, school, neighborhood) believe about God?

4. When did God become more than just a name to you?

5. Who is the person in your life who shaped you and influenced your early spiritual development the most?
   - ❏ mother
   - ❏ father
   - ❏ grandparent
   - ❏ Sunday school teacher
   - ❏ neighbor
   - ❏ coach
   - ❏ close friend
   - ❏ scoutmaster
   - ❏ brother / sister
   - ❏ uncle / aunt
   - ❏ pastor
   - ❏ youth leader
   - ❏ teacher
   - ❏ other:_____

6. What is something important that person taught you?

7. Which of the following reflects your view of God when you were in grade school?
- ❏ a kindly old man—like Santa Claus
- ❏ like my parents
- ❏ like Jesus—I saw God and Jesus as the same.
- ❏ a spirit like Casper the friendly ghost
- ❏ an angry man sending lightning bolts and punishing children
- ❏ I had no concept of God.
- ❏ other:_____

8. How has your concept of God changed? Now I view God as:
- ❏ a judge—determined and declaring right and wrong
- ❏ Creator—powerful, but not very personal
- ❏ a loving father or parent—bringing warmth and intimacy
- ❏ provider—taking care of all my needs
- ❏ other:_____

9. As a child of God, you inherit all of his promised blessings. What blessing means the most to you right now?
- ❏ forgiveness (1 John 1:9)
- ❏ peace (John 14:27)
- ❏ eternal life (Rom. 6:23)
- ❏ unconditional love (1 John 4:9)
- ❏ other:_____

10. How would you like this group to pray for you?

JESUS CHRIST

Introduction

The second statement in the Apostles' Creed is: *"I believe in Jesus Christ, his only Son, our Lord. He was conceived by the power of the Holy Spirit and born of the virgin Mary. He suffered under Pontius Pilate, was crucified, died, and was buried. He descended into hell. On the third day he rose again. He ascended into heaven, and is seated at the right hand of the Father. He will come again to judge the living and the dead."* The Bible story is about the question that Jesus asked of his disciples: "Who do the crowds say I am?"

Listen to the Bible story. Then, move into groups of 4 to discuss the questionnaire below.

PETER'S CONFESSION OF CHRIST

[18]Once when Jesus was praying in private and his disciples were with him, he asked them, "Who do the crowds say I am?"

[19]They replied, "Some say John the Baptist; others say Elijah; and still others, that one of the prophets of long ago has come back to life."

[20]"But what about you?" he asked. "Who do you say I am?"
Peter answered, "The Christ of God."

[21]Jesus strictly warned them not to tell this to anyone. [22]And he said, "The Son of Man must suffer many things and be rejected by the elders, chief priests and teachers of the law, and he must be killed and on the third day be raised to life."

[23]Then he said to them all: "If anyone would come after me, he must deny himself and take up his cross daily and follow me. [24]For whoever wants to save his life will lose it, but whoever loses his life for me will save it. [25]What good is it for a man to gain the whole world, and yet lose or forfeit his very self?"

Luke 9:18–25

1. If the typical person in your school, workplace or neighborhood were asked the same question today that Jesus asked his disciples—"Who do you say I am?"—what would they say?

   ❐ the founder of a religion
   ❐ the greatest man who ever lived
   ❐ a social revolutionary
   ❐ a spiritual philosopher and teacher
   ❐ a saint (more spiritual than real)
   ❐ an enigma (mystery)

   ❐ the Son of God
   ❐ a close friend
   ❐ a swear word
   ❐ my Lord and Savior
   ❐ other:_____

2. What is *your* answer to the question, "Who is Jesus Christ?" How has your answer changed over time?

3. Which of the following experiences has taught you the most about who you are?
- ❐ my marriage
- ❐ a divorce
- ❐ my first job
- ❐ a health crisis
- ❐ struggling with new ideas
- ❐ a financial crisis
- ❐ the death of a loved one
- ❐ an emotional crisis
- ❐ living away from my parents
- ❐ other:_____

4. When you compare your Christian life to what Jesus calls you to do—to deny yourself and take up your cross every day—how do you feel?
- ❐ like starting over
- ❐ like ducking
- ❐ like crawling under the rug
- ❐ like yawning
- ❐ like going for it

5. What would it mean for you to "deny" yourself?
- ❐ to stop focusing on my problems and think more about others
- ❐ to never do anything for myself
- ❐ to put Christ's desires above my own
- ❐ to trust God to take care of me so I can focus on him

6. If your faith in Christ meant you had to change your lifestyle completely, what would you do?

7. The central affirmation of the early church was "Jesus is Lord," while everyone else was saying "Caesar is Lord." What "gods" compete with your allegiance to Christ?
   - ❐ power / influence
   - ❐ wealth / possessions
   - ❐ pleasure / having fun
   - ❐ my spouse / boyfriend / girlfriend
   - ❐ my friends
   - ❐ my family
   - ❐ my health / comfort
   - ❐ my work / career / school
   - ❐ my reputation
   - ❐ other:_____

8. What do you need to do to move closer to Christ in your spiritual life?
   - ❐ learn more about Christ's teachings
   - ❐ have more faith in Christ's death and resurrection
   - ❐ "lose" my life and my self-focus for Christ's sake
   - ❐ be more involved in church, youth group, etc.
   - ❐ be more consistent in my devotional life

9. How can this group remember you in prayer this week?

THE HOLY SPIRIT

Introduction

This Bible study is designed to help you understand the third statement in the Apostles' Creed: *"I believe in the Holy Spirit."* After listening to the Bible story about Christ's ascension and the coming of the Spirit at Pentecost.

Listen to the story, and then move into groups of 4 and discuss the questionnaire below.

⁶So when they met together, they asked him, "Lord, are you at this time going to restore the kingdom to Israel?"

⁷He said to them: "It is not for you to know the times or dates the Father has set by his own authority. ⁸But you will receive power when the Holy Spirit comes on you; and you will be my witnesses in Jerusalem, and in all Judea and Samaria, and to the ends of the earth."

⁹After he said this, he was taken up before their very eyes, and a cloud hid him from their sight. ...

2 *When the day of Pentecost came, they were all together in one place. ²Suddenly a sound like the blowing of a violent wind came from heaven and filled the whole house where they were sitting. ³They saw what seemed to be tongues of fire that separated and came to rest on each of them. ⁴All of them were filled with the Holy Spirit and began to speak in other tongues as the Spirit enabled them. ...*

¹⁴Then Peter stood up with the Eleven, raised his voice and addressed the crowd: "Fellow Jews and all of you who live in Jerusalem, let me explain this to you; listen carefully to what I say. ¹⁵These men are not drunk, as you suppose. It's only nine in the morning! ¹⁶No, this is what was spoken by the prophet Joel:

¹⁷" 'In the last days, God says,
 I will pour out my Spirit on all people.
Your sons and daughters will prophesy,
 your young men will see visions,
 your old men will dream dreams.

Acts 1:6–9; 2:1–4,14–17

1. If you were one of the disciples when Christ was taken up to heaven, how would you have felt about Jesus leaving you?
   ❑ terrified
   ❑ confused
   ❑ abandoned
   ❑ angry
   ❑ excited about what was ahead

2. Had you been present on the day of Pentecost, what would have been your main feeling when it was all over?
   ❏ That was a once-in-a-lifetime experience.
   ❏ I hope that wasn't a once-in-a-lifetime experience.
   ❏ If the Spirit is that powerful, there's no problem I can't face.
   ❏ Give us five days and we'll take the world!
   ❏ Nobody at work or school is going to understand this!

3. In comparison to what the disciples experienced when the Holy Spirit came upon them, how would you describe your own experience with the Holy Spirit?
   ❏ much more tame
   ❏ similar to theirs
   ❏ different, but just as real
   ❏ something I can't explain

4. How would you describe your experience with the Holy Spirit now?
   ❏ on fire
   ❏ up in the air
   ❏ gone with the wind

5. When are you most aware of the Holy Spirit?
   ❏ reading Scripture
   ❏ alone with God
   ❏ sharing in a group like this
   ❏ spending time in nature
   ❏ in praise and worship
   ❏ praying with friends
   ❏ other:_____

6. The following qualities from Galatians 5:22–23 are called the "fruit of the Spirit." Evaluate your life by circling a number from 1 (very low) to 10 (very high) on each of the "fruit" in the list. Then share which fruit you marked as highest and lowest. Lastly, have each person listen while the others share which fruit they see as that person's highest.

   But the fruit of the Spirit is love, joy, peace, patience, kindness, goodness, faith-fulness, gentleness and self-control.

   LOVE: I am quick to sense the needs of others; I try to respond as Christ would in giving of myself.

   1   2   3   4   5   6   7   8   9   10

JOY: I can celebrate life even in the midst of pain and confusion because of my faith in Christ.

| 1 | 2 | 3 | 4 | 5 | 6 | 7 | 8 | 9 | 10 |

PEACE: I have a quiet inner confidence in God's care of my life that keeps me from feeling uptight and nervous.

| 1 | 2 | 3 | 4 | 5 | 6 | 7 | 8 | 9 | 10 |

PATIENCE: I have a staying power that helps me to handle frustration and conflict without losing it when people irritate me.

| 1 | 2 | 3 | 4 | 5 | 6 | 7 | 8 | 9 | 10 |

KINDNESS: I act toward others as I want them to act toward me—warm, considerate, generous with praise—always trying to see the best in them.

| 1 | 2 | 3 | 4 | 5 | 6 | 7 | 8 | 9 | 10 |

GOODNESS: I have a desire to live a clean life, to set a good example by my conduct wherever I am; I want to be God's man or God's woman.

| 1 | 2 | 3 | 4 | 5 | 6 | 7 | 8 | 9 | 10 |

FAITHFULNESS: I stick to my word; I stand up for my family and friends; I can be counted on to stay firm in my commitments to God and others.

| 1 | 2 | 3 | 4 | 5 | 6 | 7 | 8 | 9 | 10 |

GENTLENESS: I have an inner strength that permits me to be gentle in my relationships; I am aware of my own abilities without having to make a show of them.

| 1 | 2 | 3 | 4 | 5 | 6 | 7 | 8 | 9 | 10 |

SELF-CONTROL: I am learning to discipline my time, energy and desires to reflect my spiritual values and priorities.

| 1 | 2 | 3 | 4 | 5 | 6 | 7 | 8 | 9 | 10 |

7. Where in your life do you need the power of the Holy Spirit?

THE CHURCH

Introduction

This Bible study is designed to help you understand the fourth statement in the Apostles' Creed: *"I believe in the holy catholic Church."* The word "catholic" means "universal" ... so you could say universal church if you wish. The Bible passage describes what happened after Pentecost when so many came into the church (3,000 new believers in one day) that they decided to gather in homes to care for each other.

Listen to the story. Then, move into groups of 4 and discuss the questionnaire.

THE FELLOWSHIP OF THE BELIEVERS

⁴²They devoted themselves to the apostles' teaching and to the fellowship, to the breaking of bread and to prayer. ⁴³Everyone was filled with awe, and many wonders and miraculous signs were done by the apostles. ⁴⁴All the believers were together and had everything in common. ⁴⁵Selling their possessions and goods, they gave to anyone as he had need. ⁴⁶Every day they continued to meet together in the temple courts. They broke bread in their homes and ate together with glad and sincere hearts, ⁴⁷praising God and enjoying the favor of all the people. And the Lord added to their number daily those who were being saved.

Acts 2:42–47

1. How would you describe the atmosphere when these first Christians got together? (Choose two or three.)
   - ❐ chaotic
   - ❐ life-changing
   - ❐ fun
   - ❐ predictable
   - ❐ exciting
   - ❐ unpredictable
   - ❐ noisy
   - ❐ boring
   - ❐ close
   - ❐ too close
   - ❐ warm
   - ❐ caring

2. What made the early church so appealing that thousands wanted to get in?
   - ❐ the food
   - ❐ great preaching
   - ❐ the miracles
   - ❐ great advertising
   - ❐ their openness to others
   - ❐ their spiritual vitality
   - ❐ the amazing love they had for each other

3. What is the closest you have come to experiencing the kind of close fellowship that is described here in Acts?

4. If you had been invited to be part of the early church, what would have been your initial reaction?
- ❐ Sounds too much like a cult to me.
- ❐ This is a bit too touchy-feely for me.
- ❐ I have some things I wouldn't sell for anyone.
- ❐ I might give it a try.
- ❐ I would jump at the chance.

5. From your school, workplace and neighborhood, what percentage of people attend church? What's the general attitude about church?

6. If you had to rank your own church or group on the six areas that are described in the early church, what would you say? In your group, read the first area below and let everyone call out a number from 1 (very weak) to 10 (very strong) in that area.

SPIRITUAL NURTURE / GROWTH: *"They devoted themselves to the apostles' teaching and to the fellowship, to the breaking of bread and to prayer."*

We have given priority to studying the Scripture, to learning more about our faith and to praying for one another.

| 1 | 2 | 3 | 4 | 5 | 6 | 7 | 8 | 9 | 10 |

HEALING: *"Everyone was filled with awe, and many wonders and miraculous signs were done by the apostles."*

We have seen healing take place in our lives and in our relationships with one another, our families and our friends.

| 1 | 2 | 3 | 4 | 5 | 6 | 7 | 8 | 9 | 10 |

CAREGIVING: *"All the believers were together and had everything in common. Selling their possessions and goods, they gave to anyone as he had need."*

We look after each other. If someone has a need, we do what we can to care for this person and meet their need.

| 1 | 2 | 3 | 4 | 5 | 6 | 7 | 8 | 9 | 10 |

CORPORATE WORSHIP: *"Every day they continued to meet together in the temple courts."*

We meet regularly for worship—to celebrate Christ's resurrection and his triumph over sin.

1   2   3   4   5   6   7   8   9   10

SUPPORT GROUPS: *"They broke bread in their homes and ate together with glad and sincere hearts, praising God and enjoying the favor of all the people."*

We meet regularly to support one another, praise God, study the Bible, share our needs and pray for one another.

1   2   3   4   5   6   7   8   9   10

REACHING OUT: *"And the Lord added to their number daily those who were being saved."*

We keep our church or group open to new people and through our reaching out the Lord keeps bringing others to our fellowship.

1   2   3   4   5   6   7   8   9   10

7. What aspect of the spiritual life and energy of the early church do you most desire for yourself? For your church and/or this group?

8. How could you help your church and this group be more like the early church?

9. How would you like this group to remember you in prayer this week?

RESURRECTION OF THE BODY

Introduction

This Bible study is designed to help you understand the last statement in the Apostles' Creed:*"I believe in ... the resurrection of the body, and the life everlasting."* The phrase "the resurrection of the body" actually refers to the resurrection of Christians at the second coming of Jesus Christ. But this is in the future and rather than studying a Scripture about this we are going to study the story of the resurrection of Jesus Christ. The two are connected. If you believe in one, you believe in the other.

Now, listen to the Bible story. Then, move into groups of 4 and discuss the questionnaire.

THE RESURRECTION

28 *After the Sabbath, at dawn on the first day of the week, Mary Magdalene and the other Mary went to look at the tomb.*

²There was a violent earthquake, for an angel of the Lord came down from heaven and, going to the tomb, rolled back the stone and sat on it. ³His appearance was like lightning, and his clothes were white as snow. ⁴The guards were so afraid of him that they shook and became like dead men.

⁵The angel said to the women, "Do not be afraid, for I know that you are looking for Jesus, who was crucified. ⁶He is not here; he has risen, just as he said. Come and see the place where he lay. ⁷Then go quickly and tell his disciples: 'He has risen from the dead and is going ahead of you into Galilee. There you will see him.' Now I have told you."

⁸So the women hurried away from the tomb, afraid yet filled with joy, and ran to tell his disciples. ⁹Suddenly Jesus met them. "Greetings," he said. They came to him, clasped his feet and worshiped him. ¹⁰Then Jesus said to them, "Do not be afraid. Go and tell my brothers to go to Galilee; there they will see me."

¹¹While the women were on their way, some of the guards went into the city and reported to the chief priests everything that had happened. ¹²When the chief priests had met with the elders and devised a plan, they gave the soldiers a large sum of money, ¹³telling them, "You are to say, 'His disciples came during the night and stole him away while we were asleep.' ¹⁴If this report gets to the governor, we will satisfy him and keep you out of trouble." ¹⁵So the soldiers took the money and did as they were instructed. And this story has been widely circulated among the Jews to this very day.

Matthew 28:1–15

1. What angle would you expect the *Jerusalem Times* to take on the events of this passage?
   ❏ "Earthquake Rocks City"
   ❏ "Cemetery Guards Recount Bizarre Scene"
   ❏ "Women Claim Professed Messiah Risen From Dead"
   ❏ "Roman Soldiers Accept Bribe From Jewish Leaders"

2. Imagine that you were one of the women who went to the tomb. How would you have felt when you found the stone rolled back and an angel sitting on it?
   ❏ scared to death
   ❏ wondering who took the body
   ❏ overcome with grief—"I can't take any more heartache."
   ❏ overcome with joy—"I knew Jesus would come back!"

3. How would you have felt when Jesus suddenly met you?
   ❏ shocked
   ❏ overjoyed
   ❏ afraid
   ❏ full of praise

4. What is the attitude of the people around you (classmates, coworkers, neighbors) toward the resurrection of Christ? Toward life after death?

5. How would you compare the funerals you have gone to when the person who died clearly knew Christ with the funerals of those who may not have known Christ?

6. How would you explain the importance of Jesus' resurrection to a non-Christian? When did the full meaning of his resurrection "dawn" on you?

7. What do you do when you do not understand the resurrection of Jesus or your own resurrection?
   ❏ fall back on what the Bible says
   ❏ accept the teaching of my church
   ❏ go with what I was taught as a child
   ❏ accept it by faith—"I believe ... help my unbelief!"
   ❏ other:_____

8. What benefit do you appreciate the most about your own future resurrection?
- ❐ peace
- ❐ hope
- ❐ purpose
- ❐ comfort
- ❐ courage
- ❐ other:_____

9. What difference does the resurrection of Christ make in your everyday life?
- ❐ not much
- ❐ quite a bit
- ❐ a great deal

10. How can this group remember you in prayer this week?

DISCIPLESHIP

MOUNTAIN TRAINING

Introduction

If Jesus Christ is going to be the Lord of a Christian, the first battle is the battle for the mind. In this Bible Study, you will be looking at three disciples who Jesus took on a mountain trip. Follow along as you hear the story being read. Try to imagine yourself with Jesus as one of the disciples.

Now, move into groups of 4 and discuss the questionnaire.

THE TRANSFIGURATION

²After six days Jesus took Peter, James and John with him and led them up a high mountain, where they were all alone. There he was transfigured before them. ³His clothes became dazzling white—whiter than anyone in the world could bleach them. ⁴And there appeared before them Elijah and Moses, who were talking with Jesus.

⁵Peter said to Jesus, "Rabbi, it is good for us to be here. Let us put up three shelters—one for you, one for Moses and one for Elijah." ⁶(He did not know what to say, they were so frightened.)

⁷Then a cloud appeared and enveloped them, and a voice came from the cloud: "This is my Son, whom I love. Listen to him!"

⁸Suddenly when they looked around, they no longer saw anyone with them except Jesus.

⁹As they were coming down the mountain, Jesus gave them orders not to tell anyone what they had seen until the Son of Man had risen from the dead. ¹⁰They kept the matter to themselves, discussing what "rising from the dead" meant.

Mark 9:2–10

1. What stands out the most to you from this story?
   - ❐ Jesus' transformation
   - ❐ Peter's reaction
   - ❐ God speaking

2. If you had been Peter when Moses and Elijah appeared, how would you have felt?
   - ❐ scared spitless
   - ❐ totally awed
   - ❐ out of place
   - ❐ super high
   - ❐ like hiding

3. If you could choose three friends to go with you on a spiritual retreat, who would you choose? Where would you go?

4. When did Jesus appear to you in a special way? If not dazzling light and voices from heaven, how was his glory revealed to you?

5. When you are feeling "down" in your spiritual life, what have you found to be helpful?
   ❒ admitting to God that I'm down
   ❒ praying with a friend
   ❒ getting into a support group
   ❒ reading the Bible
   ❒ going to church
   ❒ getting away by myself
   ❒ other:_____

6. How would you describe your relationship with God now?
   ❒ in the valley
   ❒ climbing the mountain
   ❒ on the mountaintop
   ❒ on the rocks

7. The disciples were told, "This is my Son, whom I love. Listen to him!" What is most effective in helping you to listen to God?
   ❒ personal Bible study
   ❒ sermons
   ❒ group Bible studies
   ❒ prayer
   ❒ camps or retreats
   ❒ I think I'd need a special hearing aid for that!

8. In your private devotional life with God, what is your biggest problem?
   - ❐ finding the time
   - ❐ being consistent
   - ❐ getting to bed the night before
   - ❐ finding somewhere quiet at home
   - ❐ knowing how to get something out of the Bible
   - ❐ keeping from falling asleep
   - ❐ concentrating when I am reading the Bible or praying
   - ❐ desiring to have time with God every day

9. What kind of a realistic goal would you like to set for yourself each day for a "quiet time"—time with God?
   - ❐ 5 minutes
   - ❐ 10 minutes
   - ❐ 15 minutes
   - ❐ 30 minutes
   - ❐ other:_____

10. How could your group or church support you as you plan your spiritual discipline?
   - ❐ hold me accountable
   - ❐ share with me some good ideas
   - ❐ call me every now and then to see how it is going
   - ❐ get off my back
   - ❐ other:_____

11. How would you like this group to pray for you this week?

DISCIPLESHIP

SPIRITUAL CALLING

Introduction

In this Bible study, you will look at a fisherman whom Jesus asked to make a choice—a big choice.

Listen to the story and move into groups of 4 to discuss the questionnaire.

THE CALLING OF THE FIRST DISCIPLES

5 *One day as Jesus was standing by the Lake of Gennesaret, with the people crowding around him and listening to the word of God, ²he saw at the water's edge two boats, left there by the fishermen, who were washing their nets. ³He got into one of the boats, the one belonging to Simon, and asked him to put out a little from shore. Then he sat down and taught the people from the boat.*

⁴When he had finished speaking, he said to Simon, "Put out into deep water, and let down the nets for a catch."

⁵Simon answered, "Master, we've worked hard all night and haven't caught anything. But because you say so, I will let down the nets."

⁶When they had done so, they caught such a large number of fish that their nets began to break. ⁷So they signaled their partners in the other boat to come and help them, and they came and filled both boats so full that they began to sink.

⁸When Simon Peter saw this, he fell at Jesus' knees and said, "Go away from me, Lord; I am a sinful man!" ⁹For he and all his companions were astonished at the catch of fish they had taken, ¹⁰and so were James and John, the sons of Zebedee, Simon's partners.

Then Jesus said to Simon, "Don't be afraid; from now on you will catch men."
¹¹So they pulled their boats up on shore, left everything and followed him.

Luke 5:1–11

1. Where is the best fishing spot in your area? What is the biggest fish you've ever caught (or the biggest fish story you've ever told)?

2. If you had been Simon Peter when Jesus said, "Put out into deep water, and let down the nets for a catch," what would you have done?
   ❏ wondered who this guy thought he was
   ❏ told Jesus I was too tired
   ❏ suggested another time when the fish were biting
   ❏ politely told Jesus to stick to his preaching
   ❏ grudgingly gone ahead with the idea
   ❏ happily done what Jesus requested

3. When they caught so many fish that their nets began to break, how did Peter probably feel?
   - ❏ overjoyed
   - ❏ dumbfounded
   - ❏ terrible about what he had said
   - ❏ aware of who Jesus was

4. When was the first time you felt the tug of Jesus on your heart?
   - ❏ when I was very young
   - ❏ when there was a crisis in my life
   - ❏ in a church service
   - ❏ when I was at a retreat/camp
   - ❏ just recently
   - ❏ I don't know that I have.
   - ❏ other:_____

5. How would you finish this sentence? "I am committed to know and follow the will of God for my life ..."
   - ❏ all of the time
   - ❏ most of the time
   - ❏ some of the time
   - ❏ on occasion

6. How does the call to leave your nets behind and follow Jesus (in order to "catch men") sound to you?
   - ❏ radical
   - ❏ scary
   - ❏ exciting
   - ❏ crazy
   - ❏ fulfilling
   - ❏ other:_____

7. What would it mean for you to be "catching people" for Jesus?
   - ❏ to share my faith with my friends
   - ❏ to invite friends to my group or church
   - ❏ to show others God's love through *my* love
   - ❏ to start focusing on people rather than things
   - ❏ other:_____

8. In order to "catch people" for Jesus, what do you have going for you that is "good bait" (something that helps draw people to Jesus)?
   - ❏ my ability to make friends
   - ❏ my ability to share my faith
   - ❏ my ability to listen when people have problems
   - ❏ my knowledge of the Bible
   - ❏ my willingness to take risks
   - ❏ my willingness to "walk my talk"
   - ❏ my willingness to help people in need
   - ❏ my openness to people of different cultures and backgrounds
   - ❏ other:_____

9. What would be the greatest thing you would like to do with your life? What is keeping you from doing it?

10. How can this group support you in prayer this week?

DISCIPLESHIP

POT HOLES

Introduction

Welcome to the real world in the Christian life: the world of super highs and super lows ... and rainy days ... and balmy, boring days. Days when your prayers go no higher than the ceiling ... and you feel as low as a duck's instep. In this Bible study, you are going to see one of those days in action. The Bible story is about Peter during his down time. At the "Last Supper" when Jesus explained that he would be arrested that night, Peter said, "Lord, I am ready to go with you to prison and to death." Jesus replied, "I tell you, Peter, before the rooster crows today, you will deny three times that you know me." We pick up the story a few hours later when Jesus has been arrested and brought to the palace of the high priest for a pretrial interrogation. Peter followed the police officers and is in the nearby courtyard.

Listen to the story. Then, move into groups of 4 and discuss the questionnaire.

PETER DISOWNS JESUS

69Now Peter was sitting out in the courtyard, and a servant girl came to him. "You also were with Jesus of Galilee," she said.

70But he denied it before them all. "I don't know what you're talking about," he said.

71Then he went out to the gateway, where another girl saw him and said to the people there, "This fellow was with Jesus of Nazareth."

72He denied it again, with an oath: "I don't know the man!"

73After a little while, those standing there went up to Peter and said, "Surely you are one of them, for your accent gives you away."

74Then he began to call down curses on himself and he swore to them, "I don't know the man!"

Immediately a rooster crowed. 75Then Peter remembered the word Jesus had spoken: "Before the rooster crows, you will disown me three times." And he went outside and wept bitterly.

Matthew 26:69–75

1. Imagine that you were a reporter for the *Jerusalem Journal*, and you were assigned to interview Peter after these events. What would be the first question you would ask him?

   ☐ "So, Peter, how does it feel to be a traitor?"

   ☐ "Didn't you ever think about Jesus' prediction?"

   ☐ "How could you have done such a thing?"

   ☐ "How has this changed the way you see yourself?"

   ☐ "What do you plan to do now to make up for this?"

2. If you were in Peter's sandals, how would you have reacted in this situation?
   - ❐ kept my mouth shut
   - ❐ gone home
   - ❐ done the same thing he did
   - ❐ stood up for Jesus and argued his case
   - ❐ other:_____

3. What chance would you have given Peter after this event to make a comeback and go on to become a great leader?

4. How do you usually react when you fail?
   - ❐ kick myself for days
   - ❐ try to make up for it
   - ❐ hide my feelings
   - ❐ talk to someone about it
   - ❐ pray about it
   - ❐ shrug it off
   - ❐ admit it and move on
   - ❐ I refuse to accept failure in anything I do!
   - ❐ other:_____

5. What have you found helpful in dealing with failure, and how would you like to react differently?

6. How has failure changed you?
   - ❐ I'm more caring and understanding.
   - ❐ I'm more determined.
   - ❐ I'm more humble.
   - ❐ I'm more realistic.
   - ❐ I don't want to try again.
   - ❐ I look out for myself more.
   - ❐ I'm emotionally fragile.
   - ❐ other:_____

7. What failure in your life comes closest to hitting you like Peter's failure hit him?
   - ❏ when I strayed from God
   - ❏ when I deceived my parents
   - ❏ when I went through a divorce
   - ❏ when I "fell off the wagon"
   - ❏ when I messed up at work or school
   - ❏ when I handled a relationship poorly
   - ❏ when I went through financial problems
   - ❏ when I failed to stand up for what's right
   - ❏ when I failed my family
   - ❏ other:_____

8. Have you ever felt that your failures made it impossible for you to serve Christ again? How did you overcome those feelings?

9. Would you give yourself a "plus" or "minus" for each of the following? (Mark one or the other in the blanks.)
   - ___ bouncing back after you blow it
   - ___ forgiving those who fail you
   - ___ standing up for Christ
   - ___ spiritual desire
   - ___ spiritual consistency

10. How can this group remember you in prayer this week?

DISCIPLESHIP

REBOUNDING

Introduction

In this Bible story, you will meet Peter after the Resurrection when Peter and his friends were brought back to the team ... and restored to fellowship.In the process of walking through this story, you will have a chance to talk about your own spiritual comebacks, and help each other see some spiritual principles.

Listen to the Bible story. Then, move into groups of 4 and discuss the questionnaire.

JESUS AND THE MIRACULOUS CATCH OF FISH

21 Afterward Jesus appeared again to his disciples, by the Sea of Tiberias. It happened this way: ²Simon Peter, Thomas (called Didymus), Nathanael from Cana in Galilee, the sons of Zebedee [James and John], and two other disciples were together. ³"I'm going out to fish," Simon Peter told them, and they said, "We'll go with you." So they went out and got into the boat, but that night they caught nothing.

⁴Early in the morning, Jesus stood on the shore, but the disciples did not realize that it was Jesus.

⁵He called out to them, "Friends, haven't you any fish?"

"No," they answered.

⁶He said, "Throw your net on the right side of the boat and you will find some." When they did, they were unable to haul the net in because of the large number of fish.

⁷Then the disciple whom Jesus loved [John] said to Peter, "It is the Lord!" As soon as Simon Peter heard him say, "It is the Lord," he wrapped his outer garment around him (for he had taken it off) and jumped into the water. ⁸The other disciples followed in the boat, towing the net full of fish, for they were not far from shore, about a hundred yards. ⁹When they landed, they saw a fire of burning coals there with fish on it, and some bread.

¹⁰Jesus said to them, "Bring some of the fish you have just caught."

¹¹Simon Peter climbed aboard and dragged the net ashore. It was full of large fish, 153, but even with so many the net was not torn. ¹²Jesus said to them, "Come and have breakfast." None of the disciples dared ask him, "Who are you?" They knew it was the Lord. ¹³Jesus came, took the bread and gave it to them, and did the same with the fish. ¹⁴This was now the third time Jesus appeared to his disciples after he was raised from the dead.

John 21:1–14

1. What do you find most amazing or interesting about this story?
   - ❐ that Peter and the other disciples went back to fishing
   - ❐ that they didn't recognize Jesus at first
   - ❐ that they caught a miraculous number of fish
   - ❐ that Jesus served them breakfast

2. When you are really upset or disappointed, where do you go and what do you do?

3. If you had been Peter and knew you had blown it by recently denying Jesus, how would you feel when he appeared?
   - ❐ terrible—I can't face him.
   - ❐ panicky—He's going to chew me out.
   - ❐ defeated—I'm no good.
   - ❐ hopeful—Maybe there is hope for me.
   - ❐ reenergized—Jesus is alive and I am going for it.
   - ❐ other:_____

4. How would you have felt when Jesus served you breakfast?
   - ❐ awkward
   - ❐ guilty
   - ❐ forgiven
   - ❐ relieved
   - ❐ loved
   - ❐ other:_____

5. What is the closest you have come to "throwing in the towel" and going back on your promise to follow Jesus?

6. How did Jesus meet you in this experience and bring you back?
   - ❐ through Christian friends
   - ❐ through prayer
   - ❐ through reading the Bible
   - ❐ by talking to a counselor or pastor
   - ❐ I never have gone through this kind of experience.
   - ❐ other:_____

7. What did you learn from this experience?
- ❒ to trust God
- ❒ not to expect God to do things my way
- ❒ the importance of being in a group with other Christians
- ❒ to come clean with God about sin in my life
- ❒ other:_____

8. If Jesus showed up today and asked you to go out to eat with him, what would he want to talk to you about?

9. In terms of a weather forecast, how would you describe your future outlook right now?
- ❒ seven straight days of rain
- ❒ nothing but sunshine
- ❒ partly cloudy
- ❒ bitter cold
- ❒ other:_____

10. How can the group support you and pray for you this week?

DISCIPLESHIP

I BELIEVE IN MIRACLES

Introduction

You will be studying a familiar story in the Bible about a wedding in Cana where Jesus performed his first public miracle by turning water into wine. If you have seen *Fiddler on the Roof* you will appreciate this story. Jewish weddings were big occasions. The whole community was invited, and wine was very important. When the wine ran out, it was a great social embarrassment.

Now listen to the Bible story. Then, quickly move into groups of 4 and discuss the questionnaire.

JESUS CHANGES WATER TO WINE

2 On the third day a wedding took place at Cana in Galilee. Jesus' mother was there, ²and Jesus and his disciples had also been invited to the wedding. ³When the wine was gone, Jesus' mother said to him, "They have no more wine."

⁴"Dear woman, why do you involve me?" Jesus replied. "My time has not yet come."

⁵His mother said to the servants, "Do whatever he tells you."

⁶Nearby stood six stone water jars, the kind used by the Jews for ceremonial washing, each holding from twenty to thirty gallons.

⁷Jesus said to the servants, "Fill the jars with water"; so they filled them to the brim.

⁸Then he told them, "Now draw some out and take it to the master of the banquet."

They did so, ⁹and the master of the banquet tasted the water that had been turned into wine. He did not realize where it had come from, though the servants who had drawn the water knew. Then he called the bridegroom aside ¹⁰and said, "Everyone brings out the choice wine first and then the cheaper wine after the guests have had too much to drink; but you have saved the best till now."

¹¹This, the first of his miraculous signs, Jesus performed at Cana in Galilee. He thus revealed his glory, and his disciples put their faith in him.

John 2:1–11

1. If you were the social editor for the local newspaper, what headline would you give this story?

❑ "Mother of Preacher Takes Charge at Wedding"

❑ "Water Mysteriously Turns to Wine at Reception"

❑ "Mother and Son Save Bridegroom From Embarrassment"

❑ "Local Wedding Turns Into Wine Tasting Party"

❑ "Guests Are Stunned—Groom Saves Best Wine for Last"

2. What's the craziest thing you've ever seen happen at a wedding or wedding reception?

3. How do you imagine Jesus felt about his mother's suggestion that he do something about the wine?
- ❑ annoyed
- ❑ honored
- ❑ embarrassed
- ❑ reluctant
- ❑ manipulated
- ❑ willing

4. If you had been the bridegroom, how would you have felt when you heard about the new wine?
- ❑ relieved—I can't forget about the guests.
- ❑ curious—How did this happen?
- ❑ amazed—This is a miracle!
- ❑ puzzled—The servants must have made a mistake.

5. In verse 11 what does John, the author of this Gospel, mean by calling Jesus' miracles "signs"?

6. What "sign" led you to put your faith in Jesus?
- ❑ the miracles Jesus did in the Bible
- ❑ a specific miracle Jesus did for me
- ❑ the wrong direction my life was going
- ❑ the resurrection of Jesus and the fact that he is still alive
- ❑ the change in heart I experienced
- ❑ the changes I saw in others
- ❑ Nothing else made sense.
- ❑ other:_____

7. Right now, what is your attitude toward miracles in general, and God's working in your life in particular? What is the most exciting thing in your spiritual life? What in your life feels like stale water in an old jug?

8. What is the "wine level" (zest for living) in your life at the moment?
- ❐ overflowing
- ❐ half-full
- ❐ running out fast
- ❐ empty

9. In what area of your life do you need a miracle right now?
- ❐ physical
- ❐ financial
- ❐ emotional
- ❐ spiritual
- ❐ relational
- ❐ school / career
- ❐ other:_____

10. How can this group remember you in prayer this week?